Calvinism's Fallacies

Calvinism's Fallacies

Why The Gospel Applies To Anyone, Anywhere, At Any Time, Under Any Circumstance

NowThink!

ISBN: 978-0-9905772-4-9

Dedication

To all those who've had the pain of sin's consequences compounded by Calvinism's rejection.

ACKNOWLEDGMENTS

Enormous credit goes to my wife who for fifty years has let me be me.

Table of Contents

Introduction   13

So Many Unanswered Questions   17

Biblical Election Has Many Applications   46

Individuals And Minutia Are Not Predestined   103

Nine Reasons Calvinism Is Illogical   126

The Devil Doesn't Believe It   140

How God's Sovereignty Works   147

Election And The Case Of The Frozen Brain   161

Mercy Is Not A Synonym For Salvation   201

The Accidental Evangelist   216

Choice, Yes Unrestricted Choice, No!   222

Differences Between Calvinism And Arminianism237

Introduction

Over the years, I've had several occasions to write on the subject of Calvinism and, of course, had many vocal exchanges too. All good natured, of course, but either way, as you can see from the title of this book, and in spite of the many high profile ministers who endorse calvinistic ideas, I don't accept any of it.

I do believe in Grace. I understand that salvation is fully unmerited and that I nor any other person can do anything to earn or deserve it. But Calvinism is a very poor explanation of how it all works.

The inability to save oneself doesn't mean we are numb and unfeeling. Because I can't make it to heaven on my own doesn't mean I'm unaware of the need or incapable of desiring to be saved and a little thing called conscience is the proof.

The human soul knows there is a right and a wrong and is aware when a line has been crossed. Through repeated violations we might numb those sensitivities but that is a developed condition, not one we are born with.

If we can know when we've crossed a line, we are not totally depraved. We're also not totally stupid, which would be necessary to accept concepts like total depravity.

I don't mean to sound unkind. I actually have many friends who are either outright Calvinists or heavily influenced by calvinistic teachings and they're my friends. We get along even when we disagree. These ideas are pervasive, though, so much so that you find the effects everywhere.

A New York Times article, <u>Evangelicals Find Themselves In the Midst of a Calvinist Revival</u>, by Mark Oppenheimer (January 3, 2014) indicates that Calvinism is on the rise. To be clear, that rise is taking place only among churches that are traditionally non-calvinistic.

Before the upsurge, there were plenty of calvinistic churches already. Wikipedia lists some 200 +/- countries where Reformed denominations exist and one thing common to all reformed churches is Calvinism. It's one of the primary tenets of a reformed church. It's also noteworthy that the craze began with the Reformation and the rise of people like John Calvin no further back than the 1500's.

So, according to the New York Times article, we now have

churches not in the reformed circle adopting Calvinistic ideas. There may be no outward indication they are Calvinists but you still find John Calvin's name, words and teachings woven into sermons and lessons alike.

I don't understand the fascination. Calvinism not only dumbs down human motivation, it accords well with the excuses we use to explain our lack of performance. I'm sure you've heard some version of "everything happens for a reason." The reason, of course, is always some thing or someone else. Sometimes even God.

Can that possibly be correct?

What's the difference between "it's predestined" (theology) and "it's written in the stars" (astrology)? I'd say a rose by any other name.

Therefore, I offer my thoughts on the topic. No so much an exposé on Calvinism but a different perspective on what the words of the Bible mean. Specifically election and predestination.

Those are important words, Bible words, but they have become a tripping point for many Christians. In fact, some of the following chapters were written in response to a comment on my blog:

Do you care to address the words 'elect' and 'predestined' in the Bible? I mean, those words are in there so how do you interpret them in ways that are reasonable and fair.

This book is an attempt at answering that question.

Anyone can choose to be a Calvinist but if that is you, please at least admit it is a choice. To all my Calvinist friends, I love you. I don't mean to offend you but we are on different pages where calvinism is concerned.

One last thought. All the chapters in this book were originally written as separate essays so you will find a few thoughts repeated. I did try to remove some of the redundancy but hopefully the repetition that's left is helpful rather than numbing.

Chapter 1

So Many Unanswered Questions

God has the power to do
whatever He wants
But would He want to do what
Calvinists suggest

When any person says they don't believe in Calvinism, the
first question they're confronted with is:

*What about Election and Predestination? Both are in the
Bible.*

It's true. Election and Predestination are both mentioned in the Bible. What is not in the Bible is Calvinism.

It is also true that while Predestination and Election are both found in the Bible, and very significant, neither constitutes a subdivision of soteriology, especially Election.

Election is a word. It is used many times in the Bible to refer to people who'd been saved but it also refers to some who hadn't been saved and it never represents unqualified selections. I'll explain more in the next chapter and as we go along but for now, the word alone carries no special meaning.

The reason people ask about Predestination and Election is they've been led to believe that these ideas are somehow connected to Calvinism. Not so! The terms Calvinism and Election are not synonyms and cannot be used interchangeably, although that is the assumption at the ground level.

Calvinism is nothing more than an interpretation imposed on the biblical text. The belief that these separate ideas are intertwined is where the conversation needs to begin. We need to disentangle the mess and one way to start is to disclose the endless number of fallacies implied by Calvinistic thinking.

Calvinism (including all the concepts reflected in the acronym TULIP) is a manmade system that is not biblical, was never biblically based, and those who promote it in this life will be embarrassed for it in the next. They'll definitely have a lot to apologize for.

Calvinism's illogical ideas turn grace into cruelty, diminish the potential effect of the Cross, insult the intelligence of humans created in the image of God, and mask one of the most important truths of the New Testament.

Jesus died for everyone, every person, every individual. He left no one out. He loves the entire world and wants all people to come to repentance.

First Steps

I'm taking a good old-fashioned farmer's approach in this discussion.

To replace Calvinistic confusion with clarity, like the farmer, you must first clear the ground. Planting the good seeds of truth in uncultivated soil is wasteful. We need to break up the ground and remove the foreign matter first.

The initial set of talking points must focus NOT on

Calvinism but on the illogical implications of Calvinism. You can't begin to discuss Election and Predestination with a clear head till you reveal and dispel the fallacies of Calvinistic thinking.

There are many questions to ask and answer before you settle into the privileged armchair of Calvinism.

What is being said?

What are the implications?

How does it apply?

Where does it take us?

To be clear, this is not a study of weeds. I'm not going to discuss the ideas promoted by Calvinists any more than necessary. I'll start by giving the general definition of Calvinism so we have a base to work from but that's it.

The point of this discussion is to look at two things: the implications of Calvinistic teachings and what Election and Predestination actually mean.

I am fully aware that that is a tall order but it isn't near as ambitious as trying to build a generally accepted version of

Calvinism. Many have already tried and failed.

This and the two following chapters are long but even with the length, it's just a beginning. Hopefully, it will encourage the curious, provoke the naysayers, but most of all, stimulate additional thought.

If you prefer to go deeper into Calvinistic thinking, just Google TULIP and you'll get more search results than one person could manage in a lifetime. You'll also get a wide range of highly nuanced, incohesive ideas with no resolution or consensus. Calvinism is in a constant state of flux and has been for several hundred years because it really isn't in the Bible and is therefore subject to the whims of each new wave of super pious intellects.

A Brief Definition Of Calvinism

The definition of Calvinism according to Merriam-Webster is:

The theological system of Calvin and his followers marked by strong emphasis on the sovereignty of God, the depravity of humankind, and the doctrine of predestination.

That definition, though brief, is foundational to all versions of Calvinism.

The First Fail Point

More to the point, if you accept that definition, you're endorsing the idea that God lovingly created every person equally and in His own image but decided before the creative process began that only some would be saved and all the others lost forever to hell. The real kicker is He personally made the selections. He hand picked the ones He would save and ignored the rest.

Just saying that leaves a bad taste in my mouth.

The worst part of that idea, and the thing that makes every reasonable, sensible person question the concepts of fairness and justice is that the suggestion is that God made this plan knowing that the first two humans, Adam and Eve, though created perfectly without sin, would be the only perfect individuals to make a sinful choice that would then cause the infection of the entire human race with a sinful nature.

Let me say that again a little differently.

What's being said is that the first two perfectly sinless

humans made a personal choice to become sinners. Not just to commit a sin but commit the first sin which then infected them with a permanently sinful nature that resulted in the ongoing infection of every other person born after them.

There is an unfairness here that rubs most people the wrong way but stay with me.

If you were God and you were going to choose some people to save and leave the rest unchosen, who would be first on the unchosen list? Who would be the first people you decided not to save? For me, it would be Adam and Eve. They started all the trouble in spite of the fact that their perfect nature gave them an advantage the rest of us will never experience till we get to heaven.

However, instead of being unchosen, they were the first to be elected. That has to be a problem for any rational person.

I don't know of anyone who thinks Adam and Eve weren't believers but what that means is that the two people who caused all the trouble are getting a free pass (getting away with murder so to speak) and everyone else, all born in a state of sin, is subject to the salvation lottery.

That is what Calvinists are saying. If that were true, then you and I and every other person would have good reason to question the inspiration of the Bible, the concept of a good God (forget loving), and a reason to reject it all.

And we're just getting started. There's much more to consider.

How Were Selections Made

At the heart of Calvinism is a selection process. Some people are selected to be saved and others are left in a condemned state. The question is how were the selections made.

Did God do all the choosing, and if so, how did He make His choices?

Was there a Trinitarian meeting at which selections were made by consultation? Would it make sense to think each candidate was considered one by one and arguments offered for and against the selection of each?

If that's the case, I wonder how they decided on Adam and Eve.

Even worse. That means both salvation and condemnation are personal. God is the personal savior of me and the personal executioner for each of the unchosen.

But maybe the choices were made by lottery. All of our names put into a hat and drawn out blindly without considering any individual qualities? In that case, dirtbags and dummies are chosen as readily as the best and the smartest. Would that make sense?

Or maybe God closed His eyes and pointed a finger or threw darts at a board with all the names on it?

Maybe He chose some because He liked them better than the others? Would God make choices motivated by favoritism?

Can The Chosen Decline

Do sinful humans have any input in the matter? Do the chosen ones have the option to decline?

Everyone assumes the chosen will automatically want to know and love God but how does that happen? Are the chosen mysteriously infused with a Stepford Wife mentality? Did God create people who can't make a choice between loving God or not loving God? Is humanity now reduced to automatons?

That idea reflects badly on God and Christians.

And what about those who die before they reach the age of accountability? It is generally agreed that children who die before the age of accountability, if not saved already, will automatically go to heaven.

Would it be unreasonable to assume then that any child who dies before the age of accountability is guaranteed to be one of the elect? If they are Automatically going to heaven, wouldn't that be true?

But back to the unchosen ones.

Another good question is do the unchosen ones have recourse? Can they make an appeal to heaven's mercy for reprieve?

Calvinists, of course, believe humans are Totally Depraved and suggest that they have no ability to repent. They refer to repentance as a gift afforded only to the elect (never mind the fact the God, not just the Bible, actually commands all people everywhere to repent (Acts 17:30). Sinners can't see or understand the real issue. It's like they are dumb, mentally incapable of making an appeal, but Esau puts a hole in that argument.

The Bible says he not only sought to change the choice God made but wept bitterly with tears that he couldn't (Hebrews 12:16-17).

If Hebrews 12 were talking about salvation, maybe Calvinists would have a point but it's not. That chapter is focused on running the race of service. It has nothing to do with salvation. Jacob was elected, Esau was not but salvation wasn't the issue, nation-building was.

I'll talk more about nation building later.

Why Choose Only Some

If we're talking about salvation, another question to ask is why choose only some? Was the number predetermined, or was it decided on the fly?

Why would it be necessary to make a selection at all? What is the motivation and reason for saving only some?

Is it a question of desire? Surely, if God lovingly made each person, wouldn't it be reasonable to think He'd want to save each one? Is it out of character to think He would desire the best for all of humanity and not just a select few?

Is it a question of power? Did God decide to save only some of us because He only has the power to save a few? Is He now limited?

Did He limit the number because He couldn't make heaven large enough to accommodate all the people He created in the world? He made an ever-expanding, unmeasurable universe but heaven will have to be scaled down?

Are we suggesting He has the power to create the universe but not enough left over to save it? Oh, that's right. He's going to save the universe just not all the people in the universe.

Is that what we're saying?

He loves everyone but doesn't have the resources to save everyone so He had to choose some to save and leave the others bound for hell? He could only create a smallish heaven but He had enough power to create a hell to accommodate what some would say is a much larger crowd.

If you think that sounds irreverent, you'd be correct but what

Calvinists suggest is even worse. They say God loves everyone and has the power to save all of us but He decided to save only some of humanity and consign the rest to eternal damnation because He is Sovereign.

His Sovereignty, they say, allows Him to do whatever He chooses.

In a weird way there is logic to that statement. He is Sovereign. He has the power to do whatever He wants but would He want to do what Calvinists suggest? Does He really want to save some people and send all others to hell?

Does He really want to send anyone to hell?

By that understanding, Sovereignty becomes the synonym for mean and hateful. Is that the God you wish to spend eternity with? Sounds more like a clique. The Bible clearly teaches against such ideas. The people who form cliques are a bad influence and the people who join them are shallow. Is that where we're at?

Appealing to His sovereignty is not an answer. There's still the question of why God would want to do this? When pressed for an answer Calvinists suggest we can't know what God wants or why He does what He does. We must just bask in the grace He shows to the chosen and not worry about the implications.

The unchosen, they contend, are too depraved to know what's going on. They are eternally bad guys. Sounds a bit like finger-pointing. We're the good guys and all the others are rejects.

How Is Salvation Secured By The Chosen

How Calvinists say a person gets saved is probably the meanest, cruelest, and most unthinking idea of all: irresistible grace. If you're wondering, that's the I in the acronym TULIP.

Irresistible Grace (also known as effectual grace, effectual calling, or efficacious grace – terms not found in the Bible) is the teaching that God invades a chosen person's life with a calling that is so powerful and moving that it overcomes any barriers to their believing. They're incapable of resisting.

In fact, faith, they say, is the gift. Not grace, not salvation, not forgiveness but faith. Belief isn't a byproduct of considering the issues. It's just instilled with no mental exercise required!

It's like closing your eyes lost in one moment and opening them in a saved state the next. God is entirely the doer and the recipient is entirely oblivious.

Irresistible grace, they say, cannot be refused. Like it or not, the story for the chosen ends with an I-didn't-see-it-coming smile on their face.

When Calvinists describe irresistible grace, I always think of the film Invasion of the Body Snatchers in which people were taken against their will and transformed into emotionless, mindless replicas of their previous selves. If you've spent time with Calvinists you can't help but see the parallel.

The worst part, though, is what Calvinists say about the unchosen. Read closely. You need to see this.

Based on John 12:32 where Jesus says, If I am lifted up (referring to the cross) I will draw all people to myself, Calvinists say that the lost will be drawn to Jesus but will not and, yes, even cannot fully accept the offer of salvation. It is generally agreed that that verse means everyone will be drawn to the cross and salvation. But because Calvinists believe only some are "Elected" they must come up with a weird explanation as to what is happening beyond the call.

And what do they say? How do they explain it?

Calvinists suggest that the unselected can see the cross, understand the implications, feel persuaded, but can never fully accept. After thinking about that for a minute, you realize that's like holding a piece of meat so your dog can see it, passing it by his nose so he can smell it, and then eating it in front of him so he knows he's not getting it.

Or worse. Maybe you do that with two dogs but only one gets the morsel.

Irresistible grace may sound wonderful to the chosen but to the unchosen, it's more like torture than grace.

Managing The Forever Condemned

Here's another problem. How do you manage all the unchosen?

We don't know how many are denied salvation but judging from the number of people who don't confess Jesus at the moment it could be a mob. Even among those that do confess Jesus, many don't subscribe to Calvinistic thinking so maybe Calvinists think they aren't really elected either. But there are two problems we need to think about.

Chapter 1

One is the fact that the unchosen can never get saved. According to Calvinism, there is nothing we or they can do to change their spiritual state. They are all eternally locked in a downward sinful spiral.

That alone is a dismal thought, but it gets worse.

A second and more severe problem is the fact that the unchosen are totally depraved (this is what Calvinists say). They are born totally depraved and only get worse as they get older.

You may be asking the same question that occurred to me. How can a TOTALLY depraved person get worse? It's a good question and it points out another stumbling point in Calvinism's irrational line of thinking but we need to move on.

The important question is how much damage can the unchosen cause and how much trouble can they incite? How bad might their behavior become?

Remember that a totally depraved person cannot appreciate law and order. To be sure, they are lawless. They don't appreciate fairness or gracious treatment. They only respond to pain and punishment so the only option the chosen have is to beat the unchosen and threaten them into submission. You cannot reason with a totally depraved person.

That may be why cultures where Calvinism reigns are big on judicially regulating behavior with ever-expanding prison systems and swelling prison populations.

How else can we control this mob?

Obviously, sharing the Gospel can't make a difference.

In spite of that fact, though, Jesus commanded us to share the Gospel with everyone so Calvinists mechanically and smirkingly obey but what can we realistically expect. Calvinists say the unchosen can't receive the Gospel so it wouldn't make sense to think they could be persuaded to good behavior by hearing it.

If anything, the unchosen are more likely to be irritated by the Gospel.

That observation raises another question. Did God command us to share the Gospel with the unchosen just so we could stir things up and cause a little trouble? Is that the goal? If you are tempted to agree with that idea, you have a serious problem since Jesus taught us to be Peacemakers.

If we can't lead the unchosen to Christ and we can't change their nature, the only option we have is to regulate them. Create endless laws and severe penalties to keep them in line. The unchosen condemned, though not sensitive to sin and salvation, are still vulnerable to pain and can be motivated to avoid it by the threat of penalty.

That's the road down which Calvinistic thinking is taking us.

What About Family Members

If an individual happens to be a chosen one and he or she gets married before they get saved, should they expect their partner to be chosen as well?

If two chosen ones get married and have kids, how will they take it if one or more of their kids are not chosen? What is the point of raising your kids to know the Lord if they aren't chosen? An unelected family member can only become an agitant.

The Bible says a lot about raising kids in the right way. What's the point if one or more of your children are unchosen? The only purpose of corporal punishment in the case of an unchosen child would be preconditioning for the pains of hell.

Sounds fishy.

Calvinism Offers A Hopeless Gospel

If a Calvinist preacher stands in the pulpit and says "Jesus died for you" addressing the congregation collectively, he's lying. He can't honestly say that. The only thing he can say honestly is "Jesus may have died for you." There's no way he can know for certain that everyone is chosen.

In the early days of American history, in the New England Colonies, that's exactly what Calvinists said. They never made appeals for everyone to get saved. In fact, they never made appeals at all, ever. No one was invited or encouraged to get saved. They didn't think it was biblical.

Even though their ideas about election were wrong, they had integrity and were too intellectually honest to say what they didn't really believe.

Jonathan Edwards and George Whitefield, both Calvinists, argued over the appeal issue. Edwards preached fiery damning messages but never invited anyone to get saved. If anyone asked about it, his response gave no hope.

Either God will save you or not. There's nothing you or I can do about it either way.

Whitefield always made appeals and thousands responded.

Edwards gets credit for taking Calvinism to its logical end but Whitefield will have more rewards in heaven.

Charles Finney was another thorn in the flesh to Calvinists. He was born 20 years after Whitefield died and was an indefatigable preacher of the Gospel. He traveled and preached constantly, and never failed to give an appeal.

Finney's appeals were met with huge responses because the whole northeast of the American states had been choked out with non-appeal giving Calvinists. Calvinist preaching was convincing. Hell was made real. People wanted to get saved but didn't know what to do about it. Finney opened the door, urgently inviting people to come and trust the Savior. Thousands responded. There was a lot of pushback from Calvinists.

What About the Unpardonable Sin

Based on the words of Jesus in Matthew 12:22-32 (along with Mark 3:22-30 and Luke 12:10) it is believed that a person can commit a sin that cannot be forgiven.

The traditionally accepted understanding of this sin is that it is:

The repeated refusal to receive Christ as Savior.

The sin is referred to as blaspheming the Holy Spirit because the Spirit is the personal agent enlightening individuals to the need for forgiveness and to the fact that Christ is the source of forgiveness.

The idea is that any person who repeatedly says no to the Spirit personally wooing them to salvation will eventually reach a point where they can no longer be moved or touched by the Spirit's leading and therefore cannot be pardoned.

Calvinists don't disagree. They have described this blasphemy as a deliberate, defiant, high-handed, implacable resolve to oppose Christ.

My question is why would the Spirit of God woo anyone to be saved if, in fact, they are forever unchosen?

What is being suggested is that people have the ability to willingly, intentionally, and knowingly defy Christ but have no ability to embrace Him.

And it gets worse. This teaching further implies that every person who is unchosen will commit this sin and they have no choice in the matter. They are forced by the will of God to make repeatedly self-destructive choices that lead to irreversible perdition.

That's hard to swallow and serves to only further implicate the idea that God isn't so good after all.

And if this is a done deal. If everything was settled in eternity past, why bother mentioning this problem. Only a saved person can understand the issue but it has no bearing on their salvation, so what is the point.

That is, if Calvinism bears any semblance of truth.

Why Would God Do This

What is even more strange is that Calvinists believe this whole save-some-reject-some plan pleases God. I'm not sure any decent person could accept that idea but let's explore it a bit.

First of all, God can do anything He wants, they say, but that isn't what the Bible actually teaches. There are some things God doesn't want and there are some things He can't do.

God is not willing that any should perish but that all should come to repentance. (2 Peter 3:9)

That's a clear statement of what God wants and it's repeated just as powerfully in 1 Timothy 2:4.

(God) will have all men to be saved and to come to the knowledge of the truth.

Those verses clearly say what God wants. He doesn't want anyone to perish. His preference is that ALL (not some) should come to repentance. There's a double emphasis in both verses. He makes the same statement two different ways to make it very clear.

One, God is not willing that any should perish.

Two, instead, He wants (truly desires) that everyone come to repentance.

That's a prickly idea. If Calvinism were a balloon, it just got popped.

But there's more. Aside from what God wants, there are some things He cannot do.

Chapter 1

It is impossible for God to lie. (Hebrews 6:18)

This statement includes direct bald-faced lies and all the permutations. He won't mislead us. He doesn't dissimulate and won't misrepresent the facts. He won't fine-print us into hell.

He wouldn't tell us He wants everyone to come to repentance if that isn't what He really wants.

Another thing God cannot do is change.

God cannot change. (Malachi 3:6)

We find a very curious statement in Malachi's book, "I change not." Malachi wasn't expressing what he personally thought. These aren't Malachi's words. It was a direct quote. God said this about Himself and Malachi repeated it.

What it means, of course, is God won't say He wants something on one occasion and then change His mind later. It's not possible.

Other Scriptures also attest to this truth. James 1:17 refers to God as "The Father of lights with whom there is no variableness, neither shadow of turning."

The only thing you can do with these verses is believe them without qualification. If God wants no one to perish and He wishes all to come to repentance, that's exactly His intent. What He wants is not going to change. Fickleness is not a part of God's character.

God cannot deny Himself.

Another nail in Calvinism's coffin is the fact that God cannot deny Himself. He makes and keeps His promises. He never fails to follow through. He doesn't send mixed signals. He will not contradict His stated purposes.

And we've already talked about His purposes. He loves the whole world, has made it possible for whosoever to believe, and wants everyone to come to repentance.

These are clear, direct statements expressing God's intent. He's not going to deny them.

God CAN force His will on us but doesn't.

Acts 17:30 says "God commands all people everywhere to repent!" If people were irresistibly tranced into salvation, no command is needed.

Instead of hypnotizing us into salvation, He's made Himself

findable and knowable (Acts 17:27) and has commanded us to embrace Him in faith. If it's His will and He commands it, then it isn't something He forces on us.

Jesus wept over Jerusalem for one simple reason. They were not willing to accept His offer of salvation and protection. He wanted to save them. He was able to save them. He was even able to save them against their will but He clearly says of them, "you were not willing." (Matthew 23:37)

God cannot learn.

This idea doesn't directly speak to Calvinistic issues but it does distantly relate.

God CANNOT learn, not because He is limited intellectually but because He is omniscient. He already knows everything.

You and I, however, can't help but learn. We learn whether we want to or not every day. It's automatic but we also have the capacity to learn intentionally and we should. We are supposed to investigate, gain knowledge, get experience, and expand continually throughout life.

Unfortunately, all the talk about election and predestination reduces the motivation to do so. If everything is already settled, why bother.

Learning, of course, points to another truth, what I like to call human become-ability. We can become things. God doesn't become anything. He already is. We can become all kinds of things: doctors, lawyers, dentists, soldiers, husbands/wives, academics, and more but only if we make the effort.

We are by nature curious. God is not. Calvinist ideas tend to blunt the compelling nature of curiosity.

What Next

If you're thinking these arguments aren't sufficient, that the issues haven't been settled, I would agree. This doesn't explain "Election" or "Predestination" as they are used in the Bible. That will come in the following chapters.

This first offering was simply a groundbreaking ceremony. You have to weed out the fallacies, before you can appreciate the truth.

Chapter 1

Notes

Chapter 2

Biblical Election Has Many Applications

If you don't do the hard work of becoming the person you need to be, you won't be able to do the thing you're called to do.

In the previous chapter the focus was on the many fallacies of Calvinism and there are many. Too many to enumerate in one chapter.

Calvinism raises so many questions that if you took each to its logical end, you would end up with a book, maybe a set, not just a few paragraphs.

The previous chapter provided enough to whet the appetite and set the stage for further investigation. The fallacies, only some of which were featured in the last chapter, don't explain Election or Predestination so the job isn't done yet but they do reveal the questionable nature of Calvinism and that opens the door to a different approach.

So, what about Election.

Preliminary Thoughts

Before we can focus on the Bible passages that mention election we need to clear the air a bit. Religious folks have been programmed to think of election in only one way. They hear the word and explanations commonly used to define it limit the thought process. We need to talk about that before moving to specific texts in the Bible

Christians who've been around for awhile are conditioned to accept Calvinists' ideas but I have to warn you. To the unexposed these ideas may sound like science fiction.

So what is it Calvinists believe? From a Calvinist's point of view election refers primarily to the idea that God hand picked certain individuals in eternity past to save. If you were selected, you have no choice. You will get saved.

If you weren't selected, you also have no choice. You won't get saved.

Making things worse, they teach this selection took place before any person was conceived or born, even before creation began.

If that's true, all the important choices have been made in spite of us. We were either elected or not. Your number came up or it didn't. Sounds like a celestial lottery only in this case, according to Calvinists, God was making the selections personally.

That means He chose you in particular or He rejected you in particular but either way, it's personal.

According to their definition of election, the fate of you, me and every other person was predetermined well before any of us existed. And the decision to save each one is referred to as *election*.

What that means is that the only reason any person gets saved, whoever they are, wherever, however and whenever they get saved, is because God elected them specifically to get saved long before the creation of the universe.

If you think that sounds hokily contrived, join the crowd but make no mistake. Calvinistic churches and theological institutions teach these ideas daily throughout the world.

So many promote these ideas so adamantly that the unconvinced are sometimes a bit sheepish in their disagreement. Instead of asking questions, they walk away.

Calvinism Permeates

The problem is Calvinism, like yeast, permeates every other teaching in the Bible.

More than any other word, Election has become the anchor for Calvinistic thought. Everything Calvinists teach about any subject in the Bible is tethered to and influenced by the idea that God selected some for salvation and deselected everyone else.

Their influence is widespread enough to influence even the criminal justice system. The unselected are totally depraved, according to Calvinism, so there is no chance of them coming back from extreme transgressions. It makes you wonder how much Calvinism has influenced the penal system in the US.

Calvinists don't like it when you frame their ideas in those terms and they've produced a litany of sophisticated-sounding prose to soften the idea but when you boil it all down, if any person is not saved and doesn't get saved before they die, they were deselected or in other words, they were elected for hell.

As we go along, it will become clear why that is the logical inference of Calvinist teachings.

"Election" Is Too Common To Be Special

First, a word about the word Election.

The word Election is just one word. It isn't a unique word. It wasn't specially coined in the Old Testament or New Testament to carry a strange, weird, or unusual meaning.

The word was never intended to become a theological Shibboleth. It's not even particularly spiritual.

The New Testament writers haven't said enough in context to impregnate it sufficiently with the idea that God did something before we were born to divide humanity into two groups: the ins and the outs.

The word simply means chosen and it can apply to all kinds of things. Making choices (elections) is very common.

We choose what we wear and eat each day, what we watch on TV, what we read, think, and more.

We choose how punctual we are, how we act under pressure, who we marry, spend time with, vote for, and so on.

People choose careers, places to live, and methods for managing money.

The important point is the choices we make are always qualified or should be.

Careless people make random, unqualified choices and suffer badly as a result. Words like thoughtless, irresponsible, negligent, and imprudent describe the random-choice approach to life.

And that is exactly what Calvinists are suggesting about

God. He randomly chose individuals to save and left the rest on an irreversible track to perdition.

Election Presents Opportunities

Sometimes we make good choices. Sometimes we make bad choices. We celebrate the good ones and regret the bad ones.

The good news is after we make bad choices, we can still choose to learn from the experience. Sometimes we do. Sometimes we don't.

Choices shape our lives and in that way define us. You could say we were created to make choices.

Making choices is so common that we should be alarmed that some theological circles have used the adjective form of the word (the elect) to designate a secret, specially favored society. Using the word in that way is limiting and misleading.

We do find the word in the Bible. Why wouldn't we? Since choice is such a common feature in daily activity, it isn't strange that we would find the word and the concept it represents in the Bible.

Chapter 2

How could God talk about His relationship to humans and not mention choice? The reality is both humans and God make choices. Even animals make choices, although the range of choices humans make is far greater and more complex than the ones animals make.

That also isn't strange since humans were made in the image of God.

No human is capable of saving him or herself but one choice every human can make is to be honest about their sin. I can admit I'm a sinner. You can make the same admission about yourself.

Another choice common to all of humanity is to trust Christ for salvation. These choices or elections have happened repeatedly since the beginning of time.

We have the ability to choose God and, the good news is, there is no question that He chooses us. All of us.

The important point here is that what the word "Election" means and how it applies can vary widely and can only be determined by careful consideration of the context in which it is found.

Elections Are Never Unqualified And Never Secure

Random should never describe the choices you make and it comes perilously close to heresy to suggest God does this.

Jesus helps us out on this point. He made a small but very significant statement in Matthew 22:14:

Many are called but few are chosen.

The word Chosen translates the Greek word Eklektos, which is also translated Elect at least thirteen times in the New Testament. However you translate it, what is obvious is that the statement represents a qualifying process.

The difference between those who were eventually chosen and those who were only called is qualification. Being called is easy. Being chosen depends on one's response.

There is a process clearly represented in this text. If you are called, then you are expected to respond properly. If you are called to repentance, you are then expected to believe. If you are called to service, you are then expected to take appropriate steps to prepare for that service.

God's call should be followed by an appropriate response (believe in the case of salvation, or qualify in the case of service). Otherwise, you won't be chosen.

No one can will their own salvation but everyone can and should choose salvation.

But even the word chosen doesn't represent the end of the line. Nothing is settled because you are chosen.

Being chosen in the Christian sense is like filling an open position in a business or company. You're not secure because you were chosen for the job. Accepting the position creates pressure. Your security is determined by how well you perform, not how favored you are.

Yes, I understand that salvation is secure. Human effort isn't sufficient to earn it or keep it but what happens in this life, before you die, still counts when it comes to service. The pastor who steals, lies, and cheats may keep his salvation but he'll surely lose his job. That's the essence of Election.

Calvinism's Simple Minded Approach

One passage that Calvinists often quote to suggest that

God makes random choices is found in Romans 9. A closer look reveals that the passage does not support unqualified choice.

When Rebekah had conceived children by one man, our forefather Isaac, though they were not yet born and had done nothing either good or bad - in order that God's purpose of election might continue, not because of works but because of him who calls - she was told, 'The older will serve the younger, as it is written, Jacob I loved, but Esau I hated. (Romans 9:10-13)

A few observations.

First, this passage has nothing to do with salvation.

As I mentioned before, the word Election has many applications and this passage is proof in point. It is not focused on the personal salvation of anyone.

God was choosing the next head of the family, not someone to save. Jacob and Esau competed for the job, but only one was chosen, Jacob.

It would be super presumptuous to think Esau couldn't be saved because he wasn't chosen to be the head of the family but that fallacious idea has twisted Christian thinking and preaching for the last few hundred years.

Even Paul's comment about the children of the flesh not being the children of God (Rom. 9:8) puts no limitations on salvation. Because the children of the flesh are not the children of God doesn't mean they can't become children of God, although, that's how it is framed in every message I've ever heard on the passage.

Abraham had eight sons in all. All of them were children of the flesh. None of them were born again, not even Isaac. Born again is an entirely New Testament concept. Only one was the child of promise and that happened to be Isaac.

The choice of Isaac signified neither his salvation nor the condemnation of his seven half-brothers.

This passage is focused on lineage building, not electing anyone for salvation.

If what Calvinists suggest is correct, then all seven of Abraham's other sons were condemned to hell. I don't have the ability to entertain that idea.

This passage more than any other proves that the word Election has many applications. It's not just about salvation. It's not even primarily about salvation.

Foreknowledge Sees Everything

God chose Jacob over Esau before either had done anything good or evil but not in spite of the good or evil they would do.

It is impossible for God to make blind choices.

God has all knowledge. He knows everything that happened in the past and everything that will happen in the future, not because He makes it happen but because He is God. He just knows.

God chose Jacob before he or Esau had done anything good or evil but He didn't make the choice without knowing. And it follows that it would be impossible for God to make choices uninfluenced by His foreknowing.

According to Calvinists, we are to assume God would have chosen Jacob even if Jacob was the worst of the two choices. If that is true, not only would God have chosen the worst of the two, He would also have to do more to transform Jacob into the person he needed to be.

In other words, He would have to do more to force the issue with Jacob than with Esau.

Jacob qualified for the selection but a disclaimer is necessary. Jacob wasn't perfect. He didn't deserve the position but he had the right heart. He wanted to serve God. He was willing to learn and grow. Therefore he was chosen over Esau.

From our perspective we know that's true. Jacob was the better choice. What we know now, God knew beforehand and that influenced His choice.

God knew which of the two sons would willingly align with His purposes and He made His choice accordingly.

This was not an unqualified choice. God didn't close His eyes and pin the tail on whichever donkey happened to be in the way.

This was an intelligent, informed, qualified choice.

Why Tell Rebekah

The question we should ask, and it's rare that anyone does, is why did God reveal this information to Rebekah? Why did God tell Rebekah the elder would serve the younger? God does't often make revelations to parents about their kids and this situation is particularly unique.

God made the revelation to the mother, not the father. Rebekah no doubt shared the information with Isaac but he apparently couldn't see it and wouldn't hear it.

So, why did this happen?

The answer may be quite simple. Isaac wasn't all that spiritual. Of all the three Patriarchs, he was the only one whose name wasn't changed, which in every case was an indication of spiritual milestones being achieved. He repeated all the sins of his father and did nothing to move the nation-building process forward other than have kids.

The one parent God knew He could trust to provide proper guidance was Rebekah.

Isaac was mostly a placeholder. He even gave the blessing to Jacob unknowingly. If he had his way, Esau would have received the blessing.

God knew He could depend on Rebekah to follow through. Remember, God has foreknowledge. He knows what's going to happen and it wouldn't be strange for Him to make choices based on what He knows.

God revealed His choice before these facts materialized but not in spite of them. His choice was qualified.

Chapter 2

Esau Was Hated

The Bible does say that Esau was hated and Calvinists make much of it but there are a few things to point out here.

The first is the fact that God hated Esau's attitude (he was profane, Hebrews 12:16), not Esau's person. God is love, not hate.

But if you insist God's hate was focused on Esau's person you then need to explain why this would be true, if you're a Calvinist.

Remember, Calvinism says people have no choice in the matter. They are born sinners because of Adam and Eve's sin. They can't be faulted for that. They didn't ask for it and because they weren't elected, another issue over which they have no control, they can do nothing to change their situation.

Faith is out of the question and since they are totally depraved, according to Calvinism, they can't get better, do better or make a positive difference in the world.

Why would God hate Esau for that?

Maybe the answer is Esau did have a choice and repeatedly refused to make the right one. And God hated that.

Not only did Esau's choices put him on the wrong track but he was a powerful enough person to influence an entire nation, his descendants, infecting them with an attitude toward God and Jacob's descendants.

When one person influences an entire nation to be stupid, you've got something to hate.

The same could be said for the wicked whom the Bible says God is angry with everyday (Psalm 7:11).

Why would the Bible tell us that? Why would God be angry if He could simply "elect" each one to salvation and solve the apparent problem? Why would He hate Esau's attitude if Esau didn't have a choice?

Obviously, the logical fallacies are mounting up.

Secondly, God's hate is not absolute. Jesus taught us to love our enemies the same way God loves His (Matthew 5:43-47). However much God may be angry with the wicked, His expressions of love are intended to draw them to salvation.

Additionally, whatever God hates in an unsaved person, He also hates in a saved individual. His displeasure is not reserved only for unbelievers. God hates the bad attitudes and actions of believers and unbelievers alike.

I don't know if Esau ever became a believer but I do know that God's election of Jacob had no bearing on the issue. In fact, Jacob didn't get saved till after his election (Genesis 28) so, again, election and salvation are two different issues.

Thirdly, remember that this passage is focused on building nations, not saving souls. According to E. W. Bullinger, the names Jacob and Esau were used in place of the nations that descended from these men, not the men personally. What God hated was the effect Esau's attitude would have on the nations that descended from him.

I'll say more just now but God deals with nations differently to the way He deals with individuals.

The point is there is nothing special about the word Election. It does not represent a secret biblical sauce. Calvinists have assigned an excessively narrow meaning to this word.

And that brings us to the next observation.

Election vs The Gospel

In most discussions, Election is so closely associated with salvation, and therefore the Gospel, you get the idea the terms are interchangeable, that the word Gospel can be used in place of Election and vice versa. But Paul makes a very curious statement in Romans 11:28-29 that dispels that misunderstanding.

Concerning the GOSPEL they (Israel) are enemies for your sake, but concerning the ELECTION they are beloved for the sake of the fathers. For the gifts and the calling of God are irrevocable. (Romans 11:28-29)

The juxtaposition of the words *Gospel* and *Election* illustrates an extreme contrast. Not only are they different, the difference is striking. In Paul's thinking, there's no direct correlation between Gospel (Salvation) and Election (a calling to service).

In relation to the Gospel (salvation), the institution of Israel is an enemy. In relation to Election, they are beloved.

With that brief statement, Paul dismantled volumes of

material promoting the idea that anyone is ever elected for salvation in eternity past, possibly against their will, and suggested that Election can be focused on something entirely different to salvation.

If the idea that salvation is an outcome of Election is wrong, how wrong can it be? Or to borrow from the words of Jesus (Matthew 6:23), if you're confused, how muddled is your confusion, how tunneled is your vision, how great is your darkness?

Election Is Both Individual And National

Most of our ideas about Election are influenced by Paul's discussions in Romans 9-11 but the perspective in these chapters is quite different from the previous chapters in the book. Up to the end of Romans 8, Paul had been focused on individuals but that theme doesn't carry over to Romans 9-11 which everyone agrees are parenthetic.

The focus in these chapters is national, especially chapters 9 and 11. Every choice God made in these chapters affected the development of nations, not individuals.

Isaac was chosen to be the head of a nation, his seven half-brothers were not. Only one was needed so only one was chosen. Being the son of promise made Isaac the natural choice.

The same is true with Jacob. He was chosen to be the head of the nation instead of his twin brother, Esau, but the choice in both cases had nothing to do with salvation. We have a good idea of when Jacob got saved (Genesis 28) and it happened after he was designated the family head.

No one can really say if Esau got saved later or not. Anything you might suggest is purely speculation.

Yes, the Bible says he was a profane person but believers can be profane. In fact, the context in which Easu was said to be profane (Hebrews 12) was essentially written to encourage believers to avoid being profane, to not be like Esau.

How Does God Deal With Nations

The point is everything in Romans 9 was focused on national issues, not individual salvation.

And God deals with heads of state and national entities differently to the way He deals with individuals. You can't extend the scope of these ideas to individuals.

For example, the vessels of wrath prepared for destruction (Romans 9:22) were nations, not individuals, and the destruction of a nation doesn't require the destruction of every individual in the nation. Egypt was destroyed in the Exodus, but many Egyptians survived.

And that destruction doesn't preclude the possibility that even some of the destroyed Egyptians may have been believers.

Germany, the nation, was destroyed in World War II and then rebuilt into a different nation with the individual Germans who didn't die in the war. I'm sure there were believers among the survivors and the casualties.

When Paul said the Israelites were enemies concerning the Gospel, he wasn't implicating every individual Israelite. He was focused on corporate Israel, the national body, not individuals.

Keeping the national emphasis at the forefront of your thinking process is important to staying on track.

You could say Israel's influence was diminished (set aside) although many individual Israelites were saved.

Elections Were More Temporal Than Eternal

Another set of perspectives that we mix and match without restraint are eternal and temporal issues, especially when discussing the particulars of Romans 9 through 11.

The reality is what happens in this life does not necessarily carry over to the next. A person may be destroyed in this life, possibly due to their own sin, and still go to heaven when they die.

I've known many ministers whose ministries crumbled because of their sin. The ill effects carried over to their families, friends, and church members also. It's sad and we wish these things didn't happen but the reality is, those faulty ministers will still go to heaven when they die.

Everything about Nazism is wrong but we don't have enough evidence to suggest every individual Nazi was lost. There are many things you might question about Catholicism but you can't say every Catholic is an unbeliever.

Many rich will go to hell and many poor will go to heaven. Why? Because your experiences in this life (temporal) have no direct bearing on salvation in the next, even if you are destroyed and the destruction is at the hand of God.

God elected Pharaoh, and the national entity he represented, for destruction in this life, not hell in the next.

Don't misunderstand. I'm not suggesting Pharaoh was a believer. I'm saying that his destruction was a national issue that occurred in the here and now and does not relate to personal salvation for anyone.

Election And The Outline of Romans

Another issue to consider is the outline of Romans. Does it support Calvinism?

Romans is important because it more than any other book is referenced in support of Calvinistic thought and the most frequently referenced chapters are 9 through 11.

The question we need to ask is do the organization and technicalities of the book argue for or against Calvinism?

Of all the books Paul wrote, Romans is one of the longest and most topically complete. He covers a broad range of subjects: sin, law, salvation, justification, grace, sanctification, predestination, and election are all mentioned.

More importantly, he covers all of those topics in chronological order. Romans is philosophical, logical, and chronological. The book could be broadly outlined in several ways and in great detail but for this discussion, the following five-division breakdown is helpful:

One: Before I was saved (1:1-3:20)

Two: How I was saved (3:21-5:19)

Three: Changes that happened when I was saved (6:1-8:39)

Four: National Israel shall be saved (9:1-11:36) PARENTHETIC BREAK

Five: Conduct of the saved (12:1-16:27)

The fourth section (the parenthetic break, 9-11) is the one Calvinists focus on most but it's out of order for that conversation. Salvation, and associated ideas, are dealt with before chapter 9 so suggesting that choices God made in chapters 9 through 11 are connected to salvation is like circling back in a discussion that is chronologically based. It confuses the direction of the book. It rearranges ideas to the point of distortion.

The focus in chapter 9 is very different from the previous eight chapters. Chapters 9-11 would be outlined in the following way:

Chapter 9 – Institutional Israel established and set aside.

Chapter 10 – Individual Israelites can still be saved.

Chapter 11 – Institutional Israel will eventually be restored (saved).

To be clear Paul mentions two kinds of salvation in these three chapters: Institutional and Individual.

Two of these chapters, 9 and 11, (where God chooses people) focus on institutional Israel. Only chapter 10 features individual Israelites. Paul's primary focus was on Israel the nation, not Israelite individuals.

All of that is to say the organization of the book does not support Calvinism's interpretation of Romans 9-11.

Election And Pharaoh's Hardened Heart

The Bible says God hardened Pharaoh's heart and Calvinist play this card often, loudly and to the detriment of truth. Let me explain.

A person's heart is hardened by three things: circumstance, personal choice, and God.

Circumstance can be a factor and Pharaoh was often moved in this way.

Personal choice is often a factor and the Bible says Pharaoh chose to harden his heart several times (Exodus 7:22; 8:15, 19 & 32; 9:7 &34).

God clearly told Moses three different times that He would harden Pharaoh's heart (Exodus 4:21; 7:3; 14:4) and the Bible indicates He did that more than once (Exodus 7:13; 9:12; 10:1, 20 & 27; 11:10; 14:8). Paul alludes to this hardening in Romans 9:17-18.

Those are the bare facts of the matter and, yes, God did harden Pharaoh's heart but before you get too excited, consider the following.

Chapter 2

Pharaoh wasn't just some random individual walking down the street that God decided to hassle. He wasn't a pre creation nobody known only in the mind of God. He was a Head of State – just like Abraham, Isaac, and Jacob before him – and he represented the most powerful nation of that day, Egypt.

The Bible says much about how God deals with national entities. Many of the Old Testament prophecies are proof. They targeted errant nations.

Those prophecies were God's messages to nations, not individuals.

The question is if God wanted to direct the path of a nation in the ancient world, how would He do that? The answer is obvious. Through the leader!

There were no democracies in ancient history. The head guy was the focal point and, in fact, the Bible speaks to that issue directly:

The King's heart is in the hand of the Lord and as the rivers of water, he turns it wherever He wishes. (Proverbs 21:1)

What God did with Pharaoh wasn't personal or individual. It

was national. God was dealing with a national entity and it involved the here-and-now, not eternity.

The point is what God did with Pharaoh doesn't define how He deals with all individuals. Pharaoh's hardening was a special event that served a specific purpose. It had nothing to do with anyone getting eternally saved and we can't expand the idea to encompass all the so-called unchosen without doing excessive injustice to God's truth.

Election And The Mechanics of Hardening

As a side note, following are a few ideas on how that hardening might have worked.

The hardening of Pharaoh's heart is referred to twenty times in the Book of Exodus. Ten times the hardening is attributed to Pharaoh and tens times it is attributed to God. The first two references are ascribed to God but only prophetically, i.e., it was going to happen but the hardening wasn't happening when the prophecy was made (otherwise it wouldn't have been prophetic). It was God telling Moses that He would at some point in the future harden Pharaoh's heart. So, that means there were only eight times when God actually hardened Pharaoh's heart.

Chapter 2

In the next six references, Pharaoh is said to harden his own heart. What that means is that Pharaoh's was first of all the result of his own actions. God did nothing to harden Pharaoh until Pharaoh had hardened his heart first. It is somewhat back and forth after that.

The point? Pharaoh had opportunities to agree to God's terms of deliverance and willfully chose to do otherwise. All things considered, the terms in every case, barring the last, were very generous. What Pharaoh finally got is what he deserved.

Hardening Involves A Figure Of Speech

A figure of speech known as "metonymy" is used in references attributing the hardening of Pharaoh's heart to God. This figure associates actions and outcomes more directly than they really are.

We use metonymy in everyday speech often.

In baseball, we say that pitchers:

Strikeout batters, or

Make them swing, or

Make them hit into a double play and so on.

In actual fact, no pitcher has the power to do any of those things at will. They can play skillfully enough to achieve these outcomes on more occasions than not, and we reward them when they do but they don't force batters to act against their will. They can only coerce them by throwing pitches of varying speeds, planes, and shapes.

In the end both pitcher and batter act in character and willfully.

The same is true with God and Pharaoh. God was forcing the issue knowing exactly how Pharaoh would respond and it didn't require that much foreknowledge to figure it out. Pharaoh's obstinate nature and abusive, murderous intentions toward Israel were well known. His psychological bent was solidly formed. God didn't make Pharaoh assume an attitude he didn't already have but He did bring it to a head.

God's actions were merciful not capricious. Everyone was better off, even the Egyptians, though it cost them dearly in the end.

There's an application here, especially for democratic

nations. Pick the wrong leader and God's response to that leader may cause damage to everyone. Germans can verify that.

The Language Of Hardening Is Idiomatically Understood

Apart from Romans 9 where Pharaoh is mentioned, there's another passage that, on the surface, implies God hardens the hearts of the general population. It's found in Romans 11.

What then? What Israel was seeking, it failed to obtain, but the elect did. The others were hardened. As it is written: God gave them a spirit of stupor, eyes that could not see, and ears that could not hear, to this very day. (Romans 11:7-8)

The words, "The others were hardened" seem to imply that God hardened the hearts of certain individuals, spiritually, in an unseen manner, but it isn't quite that simple. The wording is idiomatic and therefore can't be taken literally according to E. W. Bullinger's book *Figures of Speech Used in the Bible*.

In his book, Bullinger isolates 217 different figures of

speech used in the Bible and provides many references where the figures are used along with explanations.

Romans 11:8 is referenced five different times in his book and the references involve more than one figure of speech.

One figure is Idiom (or idioma in the Greek). Idioms are sayings that can't be taken literally such as Break a leg, raining cats and dogs, keeping tabs on someone, cutting someone some slack, etc.

Every language has idioms.

Bullinger points out that the phrase, "God has given them the spirit of slumber..." accurately means He had suffered or allowed them to fall asleep. He offers the following explanation for this particular idiomatic usage:

Active verbs were used by the Hebrews to express, not the doing of the thing, but the permission of the thing which the agent is said to do.

In other words, God didn't make anyone fall asleep but He allowed it to happen.

This understanding is clearly allowed for since Israelites had been seeking God but had refused what God had offered. Their slumber was the outcome of repeated refusals of God's grace. Meaning, of course, that the choices we make are a primary factor in the hardening process.

And, God, rather than instigating the outcomes, allows personal choice to be the determining factor. He didn't get in the way. What a person wants is what a person gets.

Balaam is a good example. He was greedy and repeatedly refused God's directions. You can read his story in Numbers 22-24. Numbers 31 records his eventual destruction.

He literally got what he asked for.

Figures Of Speech Emphasize Human Response

Bullinger also refers to Matthew 13:13 where Jesus says:

I speak to them in parables because seeing they see not and hearing they hear not.

This figure of speech is called Plyptoton and is a repetition of the same word in its noun and verb forms (hearing-hear, seeing-see) to emphasize the truth being taught.

According to Bullinger, even though they can hear and see the truth (in other words, it registers intellectually) they are determined not to hear and see it fully. There's no acceptance.

The ability to hear-see the truth implies responsibility. If you can understand it, you are responsible to believe it. If you reject it, you'll lose the ability to understand it.

Hardening Is Self Induced As Much Psychologically As It Is Spiritually

According to Merriam-Webster, Denialism is the practice of denying the existence, truth, or validity of something despite proof or strong evidence that is it real, true, or valid.

The Hoofnagle brothers, one a lawyer and the other a physiologist, defined denialism as:

The employment of rhetorical arguments to give the appearance of legitimate debate where there is none.

Denialism is the foundation of most conspiracy theories. The earth is flat, smoking doesn't cause cancer, and the holocaust didn't happen are a few examples.

One more theory you can add to that list is Calvinism.

The question is what drives denialism and even more, what is the end effect?

Denialism is largely psychological. We become attached to fallacious ideas and the longer we hold them, especially in the face of significant evidence to the contrary, the more obstinate and resistant we are to a different viewpoint.

In fact, the longer we carry on in this state the less able we are to even see the evidence and the more reactive we become when hearing ideas that counter our holy cows.

That's why Jesus talked about eyes that can't see and ears that can't hear.

I can see what you're saying but I don't like it and won't hear it.

But the most important point is the fact that this effect is gradual. Children adopt the conventions of their social surroundings gradually, over time. It's what they see every day and, therefore, what they assume is right. Once ingrained, those ideas aren't easily supplanted.

To use biblical language, this psychological conditioning is hardening. The more accustomed we become to one idea, the more conditioned we become against opposing ideas. Learning things that aren't true hardens us to things that are true.

Forgetting Induces Hardening

Even the disciples struggled with hardening. In Mark 8 Jesus told the disciples to beware of the leaven of the Pharisees and of Herod and they assumed they were in trouble because they had only brought one loaf of bread with them.

Jesus' response associated forgetting with hardening and clearly indicated the condition was an outcome of their responses, not God's intervention. His remarks were accusing. Hardening was self-induced.

Why are you debating about having no bread? Do you still not see or understand? Do you have such hard hearts? Having eyes, do you not see? And having ears, do you not hear? And do you not remember?

When I broke the five loaves for the five thousand, how many basketfuls of broken pieces did you collect? Twelve, they answered.

Jesus had fed thousands miraculously on two different occasions and the disciples not only witnessed it, they also participated, and still, they had forgotten. The reality of the event had faded and they reverted to their old usual selves.

Jesus referred to that as hardening. And it was self-induced. God didn't do it to them.

Grace Eliminates Works But Allows For Choice

Romans 11:5 makes a curious reference to a remnant chosen or elected by grace and in context, this is one of the rare occasions where the word "elected" is definitely referring to getting saved. Not to the Saved but to the actual experience of salvation.

Calvinists love this reference and use it as a proof text. It is anything but.

The text says:

At the present time there is a remnant chosen (elected) by grace. And if it is by grace, then it is no longer by works. Otherwise, grace would no longer be grace. (Romans 11:5-6)

It is important to note that the election here mentioned was by Grace, not random selections in eternity past. Grace and random selection are two very different things.

It is by Grace that God offers the opportunity to receive Christ and once accepted, salvation is secured.

As the Gospel of John says:

He came unto His own and His own received Him not. But as many as received Him, to them gave He the power to become the sons of God, even to them that believe on His name. (John 1:11-12)

And, of course, there is the very famous verse that spells it out plainly.

For by grace are you saved through and that not of yourselves, it is the gift of God. Not of works lest any man should boast. (Ephesians 2:8-9)

Grace is the offer, faith is the response (not works), and the gift is salvation.

Grace eliminates works (personal effort), not personal choice.

A Word About Mercy

Mercy is another issue used by Calvinists to suggest God selects individuals randomly for favorable treatment. Let's have a look.

Mercy is either general or specific. It's never random or unqualified.

In the general sense, Jesus taught that God is merciful to everyone universally in some ways. He causes the sun to rise and the rain to fall on every person (Matthew 5:45). Both the good guys and the bad guys benefit from this expression of mercy. When the rain falls and the sun shines, every pedophile, serial murderer, bully, and thief benefits equally. God doesn't discriminate.

The context in which that verse is found mentions merciful acts or attitudes several times and teaches us that mercy should characterize the followers of Jesus. Christians are supposed to find ways to show mercy to everyone.

Of course, you need to have a merciful attitude to do that.

Any rational person has to admit that that is a difficult thing to do and even more difficult to understand if Calvinism is true. Why be merciful and loving to people in this life if those people will be eternally inflicted with pain and suffering in the next life?

That idea smacks of sadism.

Focused Expressions Of Mercy

But back to mercy. There are times when mercy is shown to one person or group specifically instead of everyone universally. There are sides involved and when one side receives mercy, the other side takes it as a slap in the face. Mercy to one is hate to another.

How can you show mercy to the bullied without mashing the bully?

Specific acts of mercy are rarely seen as fair. When defendants are shown mercy, plaintiffs feel like justice has been cheated.

We applaud Jesus for showing mercy to the woman caught in adultery (John 8) but only because we weren't there. We conveniently forget that somewhere in the background there were people who'd been hurt by her indiscretions (her husband or the wife of her adulterous partner) and hoped for some kind of penalty. Children may have been affected. I'm sure the offended parties didn't walk away warmed and consoled because Jesus showed her mercy.

The same thing is true for Pharaoh. God couldn't mercifully deliver Israel from slavery and oppression, and pat Pharaoh on the back at the same time. You might be naive enough to think a peaceful settlement could have been reached but how often does that work out in real life. The best you can hope for sometimes is a tense standoff and in this situation that wouldn't work.

There's no doubt Pharaoh would have continued to badger and bully Israel as long as he held the upper hand. Israel had very limited resources to defend herself without God's help, especially against Egypt's well-trained and mechanized army, and it would be a long time before they would develop the strength, skill, and experience to mount a defense against a country like Egypt.

All of that points to the fact that God wasn't indiscriminately choosing to be mean to Pharaoh. Israel was the focus and Pharaoh happened to be in the way. Mercy in this situation required a judgment and Pharaoh was on the wrong side of the issue.

With those preliminary ideas in mind, let's look at what the Bible actually says about Election.

Election: The Brief Definition

For Calvinists, Election is simple. Everything was settled before you were born. End of story. No more discussion needed.

I'll get into some of the details as we go but for now, the definition (the correct one).

In brief, Election has more to do with service than salvation. Yes, the Bible does refer to the saved corporately as The Elect on a few occasions but the dynamic is different to what Calvinists want you to think.

Christian individuals are Elect because they got saved, not saved because they were Elected.

And once they are considered Elect, they are then expected to expand and develop and serve in various ways and held accountable for their actions if they don't.

That understanding fits well with how life works.

When a person wins a Presidential election, they are referred to as President-Elect until their inauguration. Once inaugurated, they are expected to perform their duties well and held accountable for everything they do. Being elected makes them accountable, not secure.

Being referred to as Elect doesn't mean I was singled out for salvation in eternity past. Rather, it means because I got saved, the opportunity to grow and learn and become and do is opened up. The doorway to growth and service is now open.

When the Bible refers to a person as Elect, it is pointing out their readiness to serve and God's willingness to use them in service. It's forward-looking. They haven't arrived. Salvation is settled but in every other way they're just getting started.

In short, if you're saved, you're elected to serve.

Election In Romans 9

Most discussions about Election begin with Issac and Jacob in Romans 9-11, as it should, and most think this passage is absolute proof that God elects some to salvation and others are condemned forever by God's choice.

Just the opposite is true. This passage more than any other proves that Calvinistic ideas are misleading in the extreme. When you take into consideration the organized chronological structure of Romans, you realize that salvation could not be the focus in chapters 9-11. If not salvation, what is the focus. Service!

Isaac and Jacob were chosen to serve God's purpose. Their Election had nothing to do with salvation.

Election Describes A Working Relationship

Election happens all the time in human experience and it's fairly standard in the Bible.

Outside of creation, God never works alone. He works on people by working with people. He nudges us into projects and areas of service and uses the experience to mold us. Our individual elective purposes become clear as needs and opportunities arise.

It's a principle that was established as early as creation itself.

At the end of creation week, God brought all the animals to Adam and allowed him to name each one. That was no small task. It probably took a considerable measure of time and mental energy but the point is God didn't give Adam a list of names, He gave him an opportunity to be involved and by that, established the principle of human participation.

That's how things got started and it was the precursor of things to come.

God doesn't do everything for us. He works with us and does things we cannot do, like maintain the law of gravity, but otherwise employs the efforts of people to accomplish His purposes in this world.

A working relationship is the point of Election, not salvation. Salvation transitions us to an elected state, a place where service begins. Election doesn't transition us to a saved state.

Election Makes You Responsible And Accountable

Being the elect is like being assigned an area of responsibility for which you will be held accountable.

Two other words associated with Election are *Called* and

Chosen. In fact, Chosen translates the same Greek word as Elect: Eklektos.

Each word represents a separate link in the process God uses to develop and employ His servants and together they emphasize accountability.

God, first of all, elects someone to do some specific job, e.g., Abraham was elected to be the father of faith and to found a new nation.

God then calls the elected person to the task. Abraham was called to leave Ur of the Chaldeans and go to the place to which God would lead him (Genesis 12:1-3, Acts 7:2-4).

The next step is to qualify. Abraham became the father of faith not because he went to Canaan but because he stayed. He had doubts and reasons to leave. He doubted Sara's ability to conceive but he learned to trust God through his experiences and his faith, though weak at first, grew in strength.

Abraham obeyed haltingly because he was working somewhat in the blind. He knew God called him to be a new nation but he had no children and the place to which he was called, Cannan, was uninviting and dangerous. He didn't even know where he was headed when he started his journey (Hebrews 11:8). There were many unanswered questions.

Abraham eventually verified his calling and qualified to be chosen, not because he never failed but because he bounced back after his failures. He learned and grew.

That's the part Calvinist's leave out. Being elected to serve is God's part. Hearing God's call and responding agreeably is our part. Qualifying to serve the purpose of that call is our responsibility.

Focusing election on salvation distorts the meaning and misses the point.

That last part is where many fail. If you don't do the hard work of becoming the person you need to be, you won't be able to do the thing you're called to do. Ratification won't occur.

The order is important. Election first, calling second and chosen third. The gap between election and chosen must be filled with appropriate action.

Election Guarantees Nothing

The rub is being elected puts you in the hot spot. You now must qualify to do the job and then actually do it.

A person called to be a preacher or missionary or doctor or lawyer has a lot of work to do before they qualify. It can all come crashing down at any stage.

Being elected is a privilege and an honor but it isn't a guarantee. Like individuals elected to public office, you must do the job, or you are out.

Noah was elected to build an ark.

Abraham was elected to travel to Canaan and become the head of a new nation.

Isaac and Jacob were both called to move the nation-building process forward.

They succeeded but only because they believed and obeyed. If any one of them had said no, another individual would have been given the same opportunity.

It's interesting that Moses is notable for both his great

success and his terrible failure. He reluctantly led Israel out of Egypt and to the Promised Land but in the final lead up to the land, disobeyed a very clear command from God and missed the opportunity to enter the land.

He got to heaven just fine but he missed out on some special blessings at the end of his life.

Elijah was replaced by Elisha because he couldn't hold up under pressure.

Jonah had great success but his poor attitude prevented him from enjoying the moment and he was never heard from again afterward.

Saul, the first king of Israel, failed so badly he was rejected before the end of his reign.

David, Saul's successor achieved a good degree of success and we have to believe it was because his heart was attuned to God (Acts 13:22 & 1 Samual 13:14).

Solomon, David's son, managed to succeed on many levels but also failed badly. Israel was divided in the generation that followed Solomon and remained in a state of turmoil afterward.

Mistakes aren't the problem. Each of these people made mistakes. Some rebounded, some didn't. Some succeeded in spite of their mistakes and some failed badly. All of that is to say Election guarantees nothing.

Election Defines Your Purpose In This Life

The exact time Abraham became a believer, we can't say but whenever it was, it only took a split second. Once he believed, his eternal destiny was settled forever.

His elective purpose, however, wasn't so quickly executed. It took a very long journey and a large part of his life to fulfill his calling.

Abrahams' salvation put him in heaven when he died. His Election provided a legacy for the believers who followed in this life.

Salvation is a free gift based on a split second of faith and is settled forever. You can't earn it and you can't lose it.

Election is a calling that makes you responsible and accountable for work you're called to do in this life and requires appropriate and continuing action to uphold. It has no bearing on where you go when you die.

The one thing that is true for both salvation and election is that neither can be earned. You can't earn salvation, you can only believe.

You can't deserve election (a calling) you can only acknowledge, accept, and qualify.

Where they differ is salvation is unconditional. Election is not.

Salvation pertains to my eternal life. Election pertains to my life in this world.

Salvation is what God does for me. Election allows me to do something for God.

Salvation is secure forever. It can never be lost.

God's elective purposes must be qualified for and then sustained through right living and acting.

Salvation is the same for everyone. Jesus said: "Whosoever hears my words and believes on Him that sent me has everlasting life." That applies to every person and the outcome for everyone who believes is the same – eternal salvation.

Election is not the same for anyone. One person is elected to do one thing and another person is elected to do a different thing. The calling in both cases is not secure. Noah was called to build an ark, no one else was. If he failed to build the ark, he would have been replaced by someone else – an obedient person.

If you read Romans 9-11 with this understanding, it changes everything.

Election Is Motivating

Because Election isn't salvation and guarantees nothing, there's pressure to perform. It's motivating.

Being elected to serve is an honor that must be acted on. Failure is a possibility.

Peter, the disciple who made some of the biggest Apostolic mistakes, is the one to make this point. After mentioning several necessary qualities that every would-be servant needs to develop he makes the following charge:

Therefore, brothers, be all the more diligent to confirm your calling and election, for if you practice these qualities you will never fall. (2 Peter 1:10)

Wait a minute. Did he really say that? He's telling us we must confirm our election? We must be diligent not to fall?

Salvation is secure. Just believe. Election, however, is for service and you must qualify for that.

Elective Purposes Are Exclusively Awarded

The most important point, a point that is clearly laid out in Romans, is that election, unlike salvation, occurs when there are more candidates than there are positions to fill.

Isaac was chosen to be Israel's head of state, not Ishmael or any of his other brothers.

Jacob succeeded Isaac, not Esau.

Salvation is open to everyone but God only needed one person to do what Noah did. Two can't have the same job.

The problem is, some callings are considered desirable and the more attractive a calling is, the more likely people are to compete for it. It isn't uncommon for people to vie for a limited number of positions.

Jacob and Esau are examples. They both wanted to be the

head of the family. Only one could be elected. Jacob got the job and Esau hated it so badly that he initially wanted to murder Jacob. They managed to achieve a certain degree of peace later but the two families were plagued by bitter hatred in future years.

Three Types Of Election

There are two types of Election involving people. One is individual and the other is institutional.

The first type, individual, focuses on people who are called to preach or to missions or to teaching or to some other specific area of service.

Many individuals in the Old Testament were called to be Prophets: Moses, Elijah, Elisha, Jonah, Isaiah, Jeremiah, Daniel, and more.

Some were called to be Kings: Saul, David, and Solomon were the first three kings of Israel. They represent the full range from success to failure.

The second type of election, institutional, focuses on institutions or specific well-defined groups of people.

Chapter 2

Abraham was called to be the father of a new nation as were Isaac and Jacob. All three had the same calling. All three made big mistakes.

Israel, the nation, was called to be God's special people and an example of God's truth to the world. They have a long history of spiritual ups and downs.

The Levites were called to be the Priests of Israel.

Judah was called to be the Tribe from whom Jesus would eventually descend.

You get the picture.

The next chapter talks about the third application for the word Election. It isn't personal. It affects individuals but is more about plans than people.

Notes

Chapter 3

Individuals And Minutia
Are Not Predestined

Plans And Goals Are Predestinated
Not People

Predestination is definitely a biblical concept but we must be very careful how we apply it because, without very clear definitions and applications, it can mean anything.

Calvinists have taken it to mean God selected certain individuals in eternity past, before creation, and predetermined that they would be saved. That's the upside. The downside is everyone else is condemned to hell without recourse.

What is amazing about this idea is the fact that the

preselected ones can't avoid it, they can't aid it, and anyone not selected for heaven has no choice in the matter either. It's all predestined, or so they would have us think.

The Calvinist version of Predestination literally cuts the heart and soul out of motivation. Some won't try to believe because maybe they weren't selected. Some won't do more to evangelize because maybe the target audience wasn't elected.

Who will or will not be saved is absolutely settled completely and entirely by God's choice before creation.

Of course, these false ideas about Predestination don't stand alone. They are aided and abetted by Calvinistic teachings on Election. When the false ideas about these two concepts start swirling, the effect is catalytic. People get caught in the resulting vortex and just give up.

Once Election is understood correctly, however, which was the point of the last chapter, it's liberating. The door to a very different viewpoint opens and Predestination an opportunity rather than a restriction.

Chapter 3

Predestination Doesn't Kill Hope

The biggest problem with Calvinistic ideas about Predestination is there's absolutely no wiggle room for variable outcomes. It leaves us hopeless. That's a problem. Hope is everything. We endure momentary difficulties because we have hope. We fight for survival because we have hope. Take hope away, which is what Calvinism does, and people tend to harden, not against God but against people and situations and life in general.

Once you start picking individuals to favor with eternal bliss leaving the rest to suffer eternal torment, traction is lost. Why bother trying. All the important questions are settled and there is nothing anyone can do to change it.

Predestination Doesn't Encourage Questionable Motives

A good question to ask is why does any Calvinist obey the commands of Scripture, like preach the Gospel to every creature and love their neighbor.

This may not be true in every case but one reason a

preselected person would love their neighbor which we are commanded to do, even the ones who are easy to hate, who also may not be selected, is to rub it in.

I'm one of the chosen and I'm so much better than you.

You may think I'm exaggerating, but visit a few churches where Calvinism reigns and tell me the atmosphere isn't laced with a sense of superiority. If you're not sure where to find such churches, just look for the words Reformed or Covenant in the name. That's usually a dead giveaway, although the pervasive nature of Calvinism is such that you find all kinds of churches laced with Calvinism's ideas these days.

There's a good reason for this superiority phenomenon. When your beliefs run contrary to your actions, it makes you look at least confused, maybe stupid or even devious. You have to do something to shore up the appearance and a show of sophistication does that. If you're not BEING the part, you can at least try and LOOK the part.

Realistically, who cares how much you've helped and loved some poor soul in this life if the person you helped will suffer for all eternity in the next, no matter what?

When you think about it that way, it explains why Calvinistic types spend more time accusing, condemning, and finding fault with their neighbors. Even they intuit the futility of helping people who may not be in the select club.

Most people come from the school of thought that says no rational person can accept such ideas. No decent person can allow them to go unaddressed.

I could carry on in this vein but it won't help. All of those observations simply point out the cruel and unusual implications of Calvinistic thinking but nothing will change until we see Predestination in the correct light.

If you're not sure about Election, please read the last chapter.

Following are several important thoughts on Predestination from a biblical perspective.

Predestination Is Mentioned In The New Testament

Six different times, in fact, and in the following order:

Once, referring to the crucifixion of Jesus:

They carried out what your hand and will had decided beforehand would happen. (Acts 4:28)

A second time, referring to God's plan to conform believers into the likeness of Christ:

For those God foreknew, He also predestined to be conformed to the image of His Son, so that He would be the firstborn among many brothers. (Romans 8:29).

A third time in the next verse, Romans 8:30, in the same context, and it conveys the same meaning.

A fourth time, referring to the benefits that accrue to believers who love Him:

We speak of the mysterious and hidden wisdom of God, which He destined for our glory before time began...No eye has seen, no ear has heard, no heart has imagined, what God has prepared for those who love Him. (1 Corinthians 2:7 & 9)

That fourth reference flies in the face of Calvinistic reasoning because the object of predestination is wisdom and it is provided only to those who qualify by loving Him. That means we aren't predestinated, wisdom is and we only get it if we qualify.

The fifth time, referring to God's plan to adopt all those who get saved:

He predestined us for adoption as His sons through Jesus Christ, according to the good pleasure of His will. (Ephesians 1:5)

The sixth time is referring to the plan for Christ to be the basis of salvation:

In Him, in whom also we have obtained an inheritance, having been predestined according to the purpose of the One working all things according to the counsel of His will. (Ephesians 1:11)

In every reference, the object of predestination is never us. It is always some benefit God promises to believers and there are several.

A plan, an outcome, a benefit was predestined. We were not.

A Third Application For The Word Election

In the previous chapter, I mentioned two types of Elections:

Individual and National.

Individuals can be elected to serve certain purposes and the same is true for nations. The nation of Israel was developed and called to bring the Gospel to the world.

But there is a third application for the word Election.

It can apply to a plan. God Elects to do things a certain way. He Elected a plan that included the death of Jesus for all sinners and the sanctification of those who believe.

Closely associated is the concept of Predestination. Every person who gets saved, for example, is Predestined to be conformed to the image of Jesus.

This plan applies to every New Testament believer. The application of the plan will work out a little differently for each believer because we are all individuals, but the goal of the plan is the same for everyone: being conformed to the image of Jesus.

God elected this plan in eternity past and predetermined it would be in force during the New Testament period.

This is predestined. It's not an option. If you believe and get save, if you repent and believe in Christ, God will follow you and work with you, and for lack of a better word, hound you for the rest of your life to conform you to the image of Jesus.

This conforming process will not be finished in this life. No one will reach the perfect expression of Jesus until they arrive in heaven and each person will reach different levels in this life according to how agreeable they are to God's leading.

What is important to understand is that the ultimate outcome of the plan was predetermined, not every little detail throughout the journey.

God doesn't predestinate any person to stub their toe, or fail financially. Each of us contributes to these experiences. We're provided sufficient wisdom and instruction in Scripture to avoid many of life's pitfalls. We either get it and follow through or we stub our toe and learn.

Learning by the way is an important part of the process. It's something we can do and God can't. God already knows everything and He doesn't need shaping. We don't know everything and shaping is an important part of what we do. Learning is a big part of the process by which we are shaped into the image of Jesus.

And we learn in two ways. We follow the instructions and enjoy the benefits or we resist and feel the pain. But we learn both ways, or at least we can learn if we will.

The point is God doesn't dictate every little detail in your life. He allows each of us opportunities and sufficient space to try, fail, or succeed but always in the hope that we learn and grow.

Some will respond positively and build Christlike characteristics more rapidly. Some will stubbornly resist and their progress will be slower but God has predetermined that every believer will be conformed to the image of Jesus.

He didn't predestinate a time frame. He predestinated an ordered process: step one, step two, step three, step four, and so on. No individual is included or excluded and no one gets to jump the process.

He didn't predestinate stubbornness. If you are disagreeable and resistant, that's on you. It's a personal choice.

If you don't learn the lesson today, you'll face it again another day. If you are chronically obstinate, you may wait a long time for the next opportunity. Abraham waited thirteen years after the birth of Ishmael before God spoke to him again (Genesis 16:16 & 17:1-2).

Predestination And Breeding Go Hand In Hand

Some people, due to appropriate breeding in their formative years, will have already developed many Christ-like qualities before salvation and this obviously shortens the conforming process once salvation occurs.

Others, born in a less healthy environment, will spend more time correcting past behavior.

We have different starting points but two things are true:

God didn't predestinate your particular set of circumstances. You might be born into privilege but that doesn't make you special. Better off doesn't mean you're better.

A second truth is:

Better circumstances make you more accountable.

Jesus said:

To whomsoever much is given, of him shall be much required: and to whom men have committed much, of him they will ask the more. (Luke 12:48)

Privilege makes you responsible, not special.

The important point is that people and the minute details of their lives aren't predestined, goals are. Predestination opens the door to better possibilities and expands the horizons. It's not a fixed state of being for anyone.

Predestination Requires A Response

We often say things happen for a reason, even bad things, and I guess that is true but the reason might be different to what you think. Maybe the reason something bad happened is you acted unwisely and suffered the natural consequences.

God didn't predestinate you to crash your car, or develop cancer.

God did determine that He would work with people according to set principles and guidelines. Each person is responsible for how they respond. Some work with God's principles and move forward at a steady pace. Some resist

God's leading and thwart the plan but only temporarily.

Because this shaping is predestined, God will not stop trying to conform you into Christ's image. He won't give up. He won't quit trying. It's predestinated.

It's like reaping and sowing. If you respond by sowing the wind, you'll reap the whirlwind. It's like a fork in the road. The shaping of your life depends on which way you veer.

The plan is predestined.

God is immutable, the pathway of your life is not.

Predestination Focuses On Broad Plans

All six of the above-mentioned references reinforce the idea that God's predestinating activity was focused on directions. The only thing specified in each case is an outcome that applies to either all of humanity or to a qualified category of people.

None of those plans were focused on specific individuals. No one was being singled out for inclusion or exclusion.

For example, God predetermined that Christ would be

crucified for the sins of the world (Acts 4:28).

In other words, God predestined a plan that allowed for the salvation of everyone. No one was left out. Everyone was included.

God predestined a plan that allowed for the adoption of every person who repents and gets saved. The qualifying condition is salvation, not election.

Every believer is predestined to be conformed to the image of Jesus. The qualifying condition is the new birth. If you've been born again, you will be conformed.

Predestinations Focus Is Highlighted By Grammar

You don't have to be a Greek scholar to pick up on this truth. Anyone with a simple understanding of English and a few Greek reference works can figure it out.

When predestination was mentioned, individuals were the indirect objects and outcomes were the direct objects.

A good example would be:

"Joe Montana threw Jerry Rice the ball."

Joe is performing the action. The question is was he throwing the ball or Jerry? The answer is obvious. He's throwing the ball. The ball is being acted on, Jerry is not.

Predestination works the same way. God predestined the plan to:

1. Pay the price of sin through the sacrifice of Christ.

(God) chose us in Him before the foundation of the world... (Eph. 1:4)

2. Conform believers into the image of Jesus.

...to be holy and without blame before Him in love. (Eph. 1:4)

3. Adopt believers as children.

Having predestinated us unto the adoption of children by Jesus Christ unto Himself. (Eph. 1:5)

God didn't predestinate me personally to be conformed or you personally to be adopted.

He predestinated plans by which I and every other believer would be conformed to the image of Christ. The plan was predestined, not me. The same applies to Christ's death on the Cross. These plans apply to any person who believes in Christ.

Ephesians chapter one is an important passage for Calvinists because the word "predestinated" is used twice. "Redemption" and "adoption" are also mentioned. The word "conformed" isn't used but the idea is clearly represented if His plan was to make us *Holy and without blame*.

Calvinists argue that we were the objects of God's predestination. I would argue that the death of Christ was predestinated which made possible adoption and being conformed to the image.

God didn't predestinate any particular person to get saved to the exclusion of any other person and consequently doesn't make anyone trust or force anyone to believe. He offers salvation to everyone and the person who repents and believes will be saved, adopted and will go through the conforming process.

Christ was predestinated to be the sacrifice for sins. No one was predestinated to trust Him.

The dynamic is entirely different. Predestinations focus is never on the individual but always on the plan.

What Gives Predestination Traction

You might wonder why anyone would believe the Calvinistic version of predestination? It's a good question.

The Calvinist would say it's in the Bible but I've provided many reasons in this and the previous chapters to doubt that.

It's difficult to say exactly why these ideas persist but it might be that it justifies blaming someone or something else for our problems.

Things are the way they are because it was predestinated. God did it. It's His will. There's nothing I can do to change it.

Like the Doris Day song, Que Sera Sera (What Will Be, Will Be), we like to believe things are the way they are just because. It eliminates the need to address problems.

It is true that some things are out of our control, so there's that, but many contributing factors are within our reach. We aren't helpless.

When a person drives badly and causes you to have an accident, maybe you can't take responsibility for that but that is no cause to accuse God.

God created and maintains the broad principles, like gravity, but He doesn't override those laws every time you trip over a stone. He made evangelism possible through the death of Christ and gave us the command to go, but He expects us to act accordingly.

If someone doesn't hear the Gospel because we didn't take the time to share it, that's on us. If someone rejects the Gospel because we do a poor job of sharing it, that's also on us. We can't really claim they refused the Gospel just because they thought we were idiotic.

But sharing the Gospel widely and clearly requires effort. Lazy could be a factor here. If something can't easily be done, then maybe predestination (the Calvinist version) becomes the excuse for not doing more.

Predestination Promotes Become-Ability

This is probably the biggest fail point of Calvinistic thinking.

Chapter 3

God created flowers to be beautiful and each one does exactly what it was created to do. They don't change colors or locations. They are beautiful but they are also prisoners to circumstances completely beyond their control.

Any variation in the way they look is limited and produced either by random selection or human engineering but never by the flower's own effort.

The same could be said for trees or vegetables or most every other form of created life. Vegetables taste like they were designed to taste. Their nutrient values are preset. Change isn't possible.

Even animals act in character. They don't become anything other than what they are. A dog, as valuable as one may be, is always just a dog.

Humans, however, have become-ability. We start out at zero and work toward a higher plane. God's predestinated plans encourage this growth. He created us with the potential to become and grow and expand.

Sin, of course, hindered that potential so God predestined a plan to deal with the problem. He gave His only begotten Son to die for the sins of the world. Not just a few but for everyone.

Everyone has the option to believe. Anyone can be saved. And all the predestinated benefits apply to every person that believes.

Predestination restores humanity's created potential at least to some degree. Predestination empowers us to do more and be more.

Predestination Doesn't Mitigate Human Responsibility

All of that means, of course, that we are accountable. The law of reaping and sowing still applies. We can make a difference if we will.

Are people who fail repeatedly destined to be failures? Are psychopaths destined to be serial murderers? It's difficult to demand accountability in these cases if Calvinistic thinking is true.

Can a person be fined if they were predestined to break the law? If predestination applied to anything other than broad principles – a general rule of thumb – we would never know where predestination ends and human will begins.

It's like the law of gravity. God predestinated the law and it applies equally to everyone. Every person has an intuitive sense of gravity and the will to obey it or not. Those who obey it experience the benefit of standing safely on terra firma. Those who don't suffer the consequences.

But God didn't predestine any particular person to fall on their face.

The same is true with adoption, being conformed to the image of Jesus and receiving wisdom from God. Those who believe, experience these things equally as they respond appropriately. It's a predestined law. Those who don't believe, miss the opportunity.

But no individual is predestined in or out of salvation.

Predestination Means That Failure Is Never Final

If you've tried and failed, you have lots of company. It happens to everyone but God's plan allows for you to learn even when you fail repeatedly.

That's the good news. God's predestined plans allow for every believer to keep trying, to keep changing and to keep moving forward.

You weren't predestined to be saved but if you're saved, you are predestined to do better, be better and to grow.

Chapter 3

Notes

Chapter 4

Nine Reasons Calvinism Is Illogical

Of all moral choices, salvation is the simplest and least complicated.

In the colonial era of American history, religion was very prevalent. The first settlers on American soil were religious dissenters, aka Pilgrims or Puritans. They lived by a very strict rule of life and church was the central point of their lives.

One well known minister from that era, Jonathan Edwards, preached a sermon titled Sinners In The Hands Of An Angry God. The topic was Hell and no one could describe it better than Edwards.

In response to that sermon, almost the entire congregation reacted in some way. They wept in their seats, moaned, begged for mercy, cried out, walked around, fell down and more. That service is thought to be the start of the great revival that swept the area.

What people don't always point out is that the colonies were immersed in the doctrine of Calvinism and those early Christians took the belief to its logical end.

As I've already said, Calvinism is the belief that God alone determines which individuals will be saved and which will not, and these eternal choices were made before creation.

In other words, if you or any other person is a Christian now, it is only because God decided in eternity past that He would save you. He saw you before you were conceived and chose or elected you for salvation. God was personally and intimately involved with you even before you were you.

So they would have us believe.

In the colonial years, they believed that salvation was entirely a work of God. The Elect need do nothing, indeed could do nothing.

If any person approached a Christian leader and asked how they could be saved, the answer was simple. Nothing! You can do nothing to make it happen or to avoid it. If God has chosen you, you will be saved. They could pray about it but it would make no difference if they weren't preselected.

They didn't invite anyone to pray. They didn't encourage anyone to believe. They made no appeals for salvation. Such things, in their thinking, were theologically not allowed and therefore discouraged.

It is no wonder then that so many people responded so emotionally to Edwards sermon. If the listeners were longing for heaven – a reasonable assumption since they were in church – but were insecure about it, how could they not?

It doesn't stop there.

The logical extension of Calvinistic thinking is that anyone who doesn't get saved, doesn't get saved because God decided not to save them in particular. He knew each one of the unsaved in eternity passed just as personally as He knew the saved but decided not to save them, which means He decided they would be damned. That was the only other option.

Chapter 4

To be fair, Calvinists argue that God didn't decide to send the non-elected to hell because they were already headed in that direction. Everyone starts out on that road.

In other words, at the very moment God was choosing some to be saved from hell, He was ignoring the rest and that's OK because the unselected ones were going to hell anyway.

If God were limited, I would agree but He's not. God can do anything, except deny Himself and He clearly stated that He is not willing that any should perish. If He could select anyone to be saved, He could select everyone to be saved and the Bible clearly says that is His will.

The more Calvinists talk, the worse it gets for them.

Calvinism, of course, is not a word in the Bible. It is the name of a man who lived in the 1500's and popularized the teaching, John Calvin. Calvin gave these teachings institutional weight when he published his ideas in _Institutes of the Christian Religion_, 1536.

He wasn't the first to teach these ideas.

Saint Augustine (4th century AD) also wrote about

Calvinism, although he and Calvin differ a little, as does just about everyone who believes in Calvinism. Augustine wrote about the doctrine extensively but, thankfully, it doesn't predominate in Catholic teachings.

In the words of Calvin, the doctrine is defined as:

God's eternal decree, by which He compacted with himself what he willed to become of each man. For all are not created in equal condition; rather, eternal life is foreordained for some, eternal damnation for others (Inst. III, 21, 5).

There are several reasons the idea is illogical and therefore fallacious.

Logically, It Encourages Abuse

Calvinism bolsters the worst in human nature. It encourages bigotry, chauvinism and even jingoism.

When one nation or people group considers itself chosen, and therefore superior, there is no happy ending. The chosen are always privileged and everyone else is marginalized. The result is aggression both ways.

There are many examples of this.

The Pilgrims considered the American Indians savages.

Dutch and English explorers considered Aboriginals savages.

The Nazis were supported by Calvinistic thinkers.

Calvinism isn't always the driving force behind every case of genocide or oppression but in these cases it was. The Pilgrims were Calvinists. The Explorers were influenced by Calvinism and Hitler made good use of Calvinistic thinking to support his immoral regime.

Calvinism only encourages the natural human tendency to claim inborn, eternally fixed high or low status.

Logically, It Makes No Sense

We believe that God made each person with an amazing capacity for learning and development. We say things like,

You can be anything you want to be.

Or

You can do anything you set your mind to.

And many of our most favored political documents (e.g. Magna Carta, Declaration of Independence) promote the kind of liberty those sayings require.

Calvinism, however, strips us completely of the one liberty that means the most. The liberty to accept or reject Christ. The freedom to be self aware and honest about personal weakness and failure.

I'm not saying we can save ourselves. Self help programs aren't the answer, but any person can know they need help and can honestly confess that to God. Or refuse to.

That is a valid choice. Any person can make it. Unless Calvinism is true.

Logically, It Is Cruel

Hell is a threatening idea. Thinking you might go there because you weren't chosen for heaven is horrible in many ways.

It smacks of a partisan attitude. It encourages a cliquish, entitled, condescending, judgmental, haughty mindset. It divides people. It makes some feel privileged and proud while others feel rejected.

It breeds a smug, self-satisfied, I'm OK you're not outlook. The kind of thing we're taught to avoid in grade school.

All of that makes it cruel.

Logically, It Disallows The Simplest Moral Choice Of All

The decision to get saved is a moral choice. According to Calvinism, it is a choice no one is capable of making.

But if this moral decision isn't possible, why would any other moral choice be an option. Morality is morality whether it involves salvation or not. Why would the prohibition of choice only apply to salvation?

Also and most importantly, of all moral choices, salvation is the simplest and least complicated. It requires the admission of sinfulness, not a full and detailed accounting of every sin. No other moral choice is simpler.

Jesus emphasized this simplicity.

The person that hears my word and believes on Him that sent me has everlasting life. . . John 5:24

It can't get any simpler than that.

So if humans are incapable of knowing and confessing their sinfulness, then how could we ever make the complicated moral decisions that confront us daily?

Logically, It Excuses Tragic Choices

Here is what we have:

If the simplest moral choice is not possible then all other moral choices – all more complicated – would not be possible either.

What that means then is that the only choices humans can make are immoral. We can only make bad choices. Any good choices we might make are only accidental.

That conclusion raises more concerns.

Can we judge people for immoral choices if immoral choices are their only options?

If not, do we then excuse immoral choices?

And if we're all morally disabled, who is morally qualified to make judgments about morality or even answer these questions?

Calvinism creates a dilemma. If even the elect are incapable of making the simplest moral choice, how can anyone be judged for making immoral choices? Shouldn't we all be exempted from consequence?

You get the point. Where does it stop?

Logically, It's Confusing

Every challenge against Calvinism is met with by an unending, twisting, tangled maze of arguments. Keeping track of each argument and how they interconnect is like playing fifteen games of chess simultaneously.

Very few people can do that.

You're not going to understand this. No one really figures it out. Many Calvinistic thinkers even admit that the only thing you can do is acquiesce.

Calvinists spend inordinate amounts of time explaining why "World" doesn't mean everyone and why God's desire that all men come to the knowledge of the truth doesn't really apply to all men.

Calvinists say that God wants everyone to know the truth but only allows some to embrace it! Does that make sense?

If you weren't confused before, you will be.

The Bible is God's simple message of salvation. You don't need a degree to figure it out, but you'll need one to get your head around Calvinism.

Logically, It Contradicts What The Bible Says

A few of the verses Calvinists have written volumes to explain, or maybe I should say correct, follow:

(God) will have all men to be saved and to come to the knowledge of the truth. 1 Timothy 2:4

And

The Lord is not. . .willing that any should perish but that all should come to repentance. 2 Peter 3:9

And

For whosoever shall call upon the name of the Lord shall be saved. Romans 10:13

That's just a few. There are more.

If someone were to ask you how to be saved what would you tell them? Would it be legitimate to quote Romans 10:13, "whosoever shall call shall be saved" or should we douse their interest with an answer like "no one can know till God saves them."

Either the Bible can be taken literally or not. Calvinism shouldn't be allowed to stand in the way of that understanding.

Logically, It Encourages Christians To Lie

We are commanded to preach the Gospel to everyone. Jesus plainly said:

Go into all the world and preach the Gospel to every creature. Mark 16:15

But that means Jesus is commanding us to lie. If only some are elected and we present the Gospel to everyone, then we are bound to tell some of the non-elect that they can be saved when they can't.

If Calvinists don't qualify the Gospel message – it is good news only for the elect – then we are knowingly misleading the non-elect, which is the same as lying.

Would Jesus really tell us to do that?

All These Observations Makes Calvinism Unfair

Yes, God can do anything He wants but I can't imagine any scenario in which He would want Calvinism. It isn't fair and goes against everything the Bible says about God.

Chapter 4

Notes

Chapter 5

The Devil Doesn't Believe It

Sinners Are Born Sullied Not Senseless

The Devil doesn't believe Calvinism but he sure things it's a good idea and why not? One of his tricks is to make people think they can't get saved, so anything that encourages doubt works right into his hands.

But, even though he thinks Calvinism is a good idea he doesn't believe it. He wants people to believe God selected certain individuals to save and consigned everyone else to hell and those choices were all made before creation.

If you think Calvinism doesn't make sense, you're correct,

unless you're the Devil. He doesn't want people to get saved and will do anything he can to thwart the process.

Ignorance, of course, is one strategy. If a person doesn't know the Gospel, they won't believe the Gospel (how can they believe in Him in Whom they have not heard, Rom. 10:14).

But ignorance is only one strategy. The Gospel is pervasive. It's everywhere so another strategy is needed. And what might that be? Confuse the issue. Let people have the Gospel but give it a twist. One way to do that is convince people that it may not apply to them. What better way to do that than Calvinism.

And you find Calvinism everywhere you find the Gospel.

But, getting back to my original thought, the Devil doesn't buy it. Not only does he focus on EVERY person – not just the elect or non-elect – he also works to blind them all to the truth of the Gospel – a condition Calvinists suggest already exists and is curable only by a special, mystical, enabling by God.

Instead, however, the Bible says the following:

But IF (emphasis mine) our gospel is hidden, it is hidden to them that are lost, in whom the god of this world (the Devil) has blinded the minds of them which believe not... (2 Corinthians 4:3-4)

The word "IF" strongly suggests that blindness is a manufactured state. It is the result of conditioning over time. You aren't born that way, you become that way. It is not universal. It is a developed condition, which means we are born sinners not senseless.

Additionally, a sin nature alone is not enough to blind us. The Devil wouldn't work to blind us if the condition already existed. In fact, the above verse describes the Devil's actions and if actions, rather than words, determine what a person really believes then based on this verse:

He believes no person is "Unconditionally Elected" for salvation.

Obviously, if he believed certain people were irresistibly and unconditionally chosen to be saved he wouldn't work so hard to interfere, as this verse implies. He may be deluded but he isn't stupid. Why try blocking what cannot be altered.

It's also fair to say he believes no one is destined for hell.

Chapter 5

When Felix trembled (Acts 24:25) and Agrippa was almost persuaded (Acts 26:28) and countless others were moved by the truth of the Gospel the Devil reacted. He didn't assume these people were pre-chosen for hell but rather, worriedly got in the way, doing anything he could to prevent them hearing the Gospel in the first place and interfering with their believing if they did.

According to Calvinism, anyone pre-elected for hell is already in the bag. Why would he worry about them? And anyone pre-elected for heaven can never be dissuaded. Why would he worry about them? If Calvinism is true he obviously missed the point.

The truth is he doesn't believe people are naturally blinded to the Gospel or incapable of grasping it. One way he can obstruct the mission is to promote Calvinism.

Yes, people are blinded to the Gospel but their blindness is not due to their sinful condition. The Bible plainly says,

The god of this world (the Devil) has blinded the minds of unbelievers...

Not only does the Bible say the Devil causes this blindness but there is also a lot of evidence to prove this blindness is not permanent. Felix trembled, Agrippa was almost persuaded and Paul – and others – were stoned, beaten, run out of town and executed by those who heard the Gospel, not because they couldn't understand it but because they did.

Satan can't prevent people from hearing the Gospel or believing the Gospel so he works to keep them from understanding the Gospel. It really is for everyone and he hates that.

Conclusion

These are controversial ideas, yes, but only because Calvinism is entrenched. If Calvinism is true, you have many questions to answer.

Why doesn't the Devil believe it?

How do you keep Calvinistic Christians from developing a smug "insider" attitude?

What purpose is served when unbelievers hear these ideas since you can't know who is or is not elected?

How can we justify preaching anything that might discourage "belief?"

How can we be comfortable explaining any doctrine with statements like, "God can do whatever He wants," which makes Him seem capricious?

And these are just a few questions that come to mind.

Maybe this is one issue about which we should agree with the Devil.

Notes

Chapter 6

How God's Sovereignty Works

As Omnipotent, God possesses all power
As Sovereign, He shares it

Sovereignty implies relationship and is often defined in terms of control, i.e., how much control the Sovereign – in this case God – exerts over His subjects. Obviously, God as Sovereign has absolute authority – He is still all powerful – but He has chosen not to exercise that authority absolutely. Control is a part of the picture but it's not central.

Omnipotence is power without limits, shape or application. God has always had "all power" but before creation it was only an unexpressed attribute. It couldn't be measured, categorized or used by others.

Before creation there was no one else to use it.

Designing and assembling the created order changed all that. Power management – sovereignty – became an issue after creation and it involves more than one person. In fact, it involves every person.

There are many power processes neglected, abused or well managed only by humans:

We maintain the garden - ecology.

We maintain emotional health - sociology.

We maintain physical health - medicine.

We maintain safe living conditions - civil engineering.

We maintain moral safety - jurisprudence

Or not…

God created vegetation and maintains the laws of agriculture but delegates garden maintenance, along with many other responsibilities, to humans.

Following creation, He sovereignly maintains the natural processes that are foundational to the balance and beauty of the created realm. But His sovereignty isn't equivalent to absolute control. We have responsibilities to fulfill and decisions to make and there are natural consequences for neglecting those responsibilities.

We either manage these power processes reliably and benefit, or neglect them and lose but God's sovereignty doesn't imply divine interference or intrusion every time we make a mess or fail to perform. We're still suffering the consequences of Adam and Eve's poor choices in the garden.

Sovereignty does not override human-will. On the contrary, it allows for it. Since God is the one who established human-will, we have no reason to believe He is exercising absolute control over our choices. Sovereignty and personal choice neither contradict nor compete.

This applies as much to spiritual laws as it does to any other. God sovereignly made salvation possible and we, through choice, accept or reject it. Sovereignty allows for human choice. There's no zero sum relationship between these two concepts. One doesn't win if the other loses. One isn't "on" when the other is "off." The effect of the two is catalyzing not neutralizing. They can both be active simultaneously in the service of God's will. There's no cancelling effect either way.

But this explanation of sovereignty is not commonly accepted and the topic is by nature controversial and often misunderstood.

There are some – Calvinists – who mistakenly believe that God chooses who will and will not get saved. He made these choices in eternity past, they say, and there is no human response that can change it. In fact, they don't think repentance is possible unless God sovereignly allows it.

The negative but logical inference is quite ugly. If God didn't choose a person to go to heaven then He obviously chose to send them to hell. Grim thought and Calvinists respond with all kinds of defensive – or dismissive – arguments but I won't waste time sharing or discussing them here. It's all just a lot of smoke screening – academic camouflaging.

One chapter in the Bible which is often invoked to suggest that God's sovereignty completely overrides man's will, especially with regard to salvation, is Romans chapter nine.

The problem is, Romans 9 has nothing to do with personal, individual salvation. In fact, chapters 9 through 11 are focused on the choices God made in the process of developing the plan of salvation, which involved the nation of salvation, Israel.

These chapters are not discussing the salvation of any particular person and the technical structure of the book is proof.

The first three chapters develop the universal human need for salvation.

Chapter 4 describes the required human response to God's offer of salvation, faith.

Chapter 5 discusses the benefit of salvation, peace with God.

Chapters 6 through 8 discusses the nature of the saved person as compared to that of a lost person, new and conforming to the image of Christ.

By the time we get to chapter 9 we are long past personal salvation and Paul begins discussing the choices God made in the process of providing the plan of salvation.

But an important question is being raised and answered in the these three chapters (9-11), which is: "What is happening with the nation of Israel?"

What part did Israel play in the past and what part do they play in the present scheme of things? Has God set them aside temporarily or has He refused them forever?

These questions were important to Jewish Christians. It was obvious God had transitioned to a Gentile base of operation and they were insecure about this. In these chapters, Paul explained that God's calling on Israel through Abraham was irrevocable even though the plan had been unexpectedly changed for a period (Romans 11:29). He emphatically asked and answered the very question that bothered them:

Has God rejected His people? Absolutely not! (Romans 11:1)

The truth is, God "elected" Israel, the nation, to serve certain eternal purposes and those purposes would be realized even if some individual Israelites spiritually balked thus pointing to the fact that these chapters were focused on "national" issues not personal ones. Jewish Christians were asking about the salvation of the nation of Israel not other Jewish individuals.

To reassure them, and to emphasize this point, Paul highlighted the strategic decisions God made in the development of Israel and how it led to a salvation made possible for all.

One very subtle point is often missed when discussing these chapters. Service is the context not Salvation. The individuals named in this passage were being chosen by God to SERVE specific purposes in this life not get saved for the next. And this context trumps any discussion of individual salvation. The proofs are many:

He is talking about a nation – an institution – Israel. Institutions are things, humans are not. Humans do serve God but that service has no bearing on individual salvation. Israel, the institution, according to Romans 11:26, will be saved even though many individual Israelites won't be. That represents a huge contradiction for anyone wishing to connect God's irrevocable callings to eternal salvation. This passage is addressing institutional not personal issues.

The individuals God "called" in these chapters represented mile stones in the development of this nation. These "callings" did not signal the salvation or reprobation of any person. Isaac, Jacob and even Pharaoh represented critical "elections" in this process.

Election, of course, as I've mentioned before, refers to service not salvation. Pharaoh was chosen for destruction in this life not hell in the next. Hardening made him delusional to the practical wisdom of dealing with a potentially destructive foreign affair. God's actions were focused on Pharaoh's kingdom not his soul. Yes, he was elected but his election had nothing to do with salvation and everything to do with service. *

Also, Paul made it very clear that Israel's Election – service – was totally separate to the Gospel: "As concerning the Gospel, they (Israel) are enemies for your sakes, but as touching the election, they are beloved for the Father's sake." (Romans 11:28).

Conditions are placed on these callings. Israel was cut out of service (off the vine) and the Gentiles were called into service (grafted into the vine) in their place, temporarily. Neither group deserved the calling, although to keep it they had to qualify (Romans 11:22-24). Many are called, few are chosen.

Salvation, on the other hand, is very different to a calling. Other than faith in Christ, it has no conditions and anyone can express faith. And once saved you can't be lost. A calling can be lost, either by stubbornly refusing it or managing it carelessly but salvation can never be lost.

The only portion of these chapters discussing individual eternal salvation makes it clear that anyone can call on Christ and when they do they will be saved (Romans 10:13). The only thing prompting a person to call is hearing the Gospel message (Romans 10:14 & 17).

These chapters are discussing Israel as an institution not the salvation of any person and even though a few individuals are named, they only represent markers who influenced the development of the nation.

Paul gives us a very brief history of this nation's development in which he focuses on three major events – involving sovereign choices by God – which in turn led to the spiritual and influential expansion of the nation.

These choices involved people and we often assume that a selection implies the absolute acceptance of one person and the absolute rejection of another. Not so. David was chosen to be King over Israel but he wasn't the only choice nor was he always kingly. David was chosen for reasons about which we can only speculate. His relationship to God was strong and he was humble but I doubt he was the only one to qualify in that way. But his calling wasn't about his salvation and it certainly wasn't accompanied by any exclusion clauses regarding any other potential candidates.

ISHMAEL AND ISAAC

That brings us to the first couple of events mentioned in Romans 9 both of which involved a strategic choice between two sets of sons: Isaac or Ishmael and Jacob or Esau.

Ishmael and Isaac were half brothers, same father different mothers. The "different mothers" part is another story. For now Paul is focusing on one question: why did Isaac inherit the promise and Ishmael not? Neither descendant did anything to deserve it.

Obviously, the promises outlived Abraham by many centuries and were developed through many generations.

The foundational promise was Abraham was to become the father of many nations, a goal that couldn't be reached in one life time. Even Solomon with numerous wives and concubines couldn't accomplish that.

The ultimate promise was a Redeemer would eventually descend through Abraham's line.

The promise was made to one generation and passed down through many. The big question at every mile stone was, who is the next recipient?

Sometimes the choices were made for obvious reasons, but only by God, and sometimes human will and character were factors.

The reason God chose Isaac instead of Ishmael is a no-brainer. It wasn't due to any credit or fault either way. Isaac was the child of choice because he was the child of promise. He was the living reminder that God keeps His promises.

Choosing Isaac did not reflect negatively on Ishmael or positively on Isaac. It was the natural outgrowth of God's plan, the obvious choice. God didn't reject Ishmael for this calling any more than He rejected every other person. If Sara had given birth to a second boy after Isaac, he would have been rejected also. Obviously, that didn't happen but logically the point stands.

The choice in this matter involved the line of succession not the salvation of any person. It was aimed at service not salvation and answers the question, "Who would have the honor of serving God's purpose in this matter?"

There is nothing suggesting that:

1. The subsequent revelation given to Israel would not be accessible to Ishmaelites.

2. Jesus being born to Israelite lineage would disregard Ishmaelites.

3. The choice of one automatically signaled the eternal damnation of the other with no regard to personal response.

God made a sovereign choice between Ishmael and Isaac about the line of succession and it really wasn't difficult to see why. Reading any implications about personal salvation into the text not only distorts the meaning but implies all sorts of abusive ideas about who can or can't get saved.

Neither Ishmael being born of a polygamous relationship nor Isaac being the promised son has any bearing on the salvation of either. To suggest it, is almost criminal.

We'll talk about Jacob and Esau in a different chapter.

_____

* Pharaoh probably died in unbelief but that wasn't the point in Romans 9. Pharaoh had hardened himself to eternal issues long

Chapter 6

before his meeting with Moses. In the Exodus, he was hardened
to the good sense of "letting God's people go."

Notes

Chapter 7

Election And The Case Of The Frozen Brain

Election Is In The Bible But It's Not What You Think

Question 7 of the Westminster Short Catechism asks: What are the decrees of God?

I guess it's a good question but the catechism gives no indication as to why they ask or why it's important. Seems a bit mysterious.

I'm curious as to why they mention "Decrees" at all. The word doesn't feature widely in the Old or New Testaments so you're left wondering, but not for long. The catechism's answer to this strange question takes a huge leap from the mysteriously broad to the philosophically outrageous:

The decrees of God are His eternal purpose, according to the counsel of His will, whereby, for His own glory, He hath FOREORDAINED WHATSOEVER COMES TO PASS.

The answer gets right to the point but instead of clearing the air, it leaves you confused and fretful, not to mention shocked!

Did they really say God ordained "Whatsoever comes to pass?"

If you're a thinking person and you extend this short statement to its logical end, many difficult questions arise. So many, in fact, that the brain freezes up like a PC. It becomes a hailstorm of inquiry.

Did God really foreordain murder, mayhem, genocide, abuse, corruption, oppression, natural catastrophe and so on? The inferred meaning is impossible to miss. It's also difficult to accept.

It really boils down to just one question. Are horrible things really a part of God's will and has His personal counsel guided events to such conclusions?

And if the answer to that question is yes, you are compelled to ask an additional question. How can these horrible things possibly glorify God?

That's what the catechism says. He *decreed* everything that happens for His own glory.

For most people that doesn't make sense but amazingly, and in spite of the logical implications, those who hold these beliefs are unfazed. The unfortunate but unequivocal response to "Are you sure about this" is "Yes! Everything that happens is in sync with God's predetermined will!"

And if in the interest of clarity you should inquire further, the rationale becomes a bit circular.

Everything happens and is foreordained by God in order to serve His eternal purpose and to glorify Himself, and because it is for His own glory, it's all arranged by the counsel of His own will!!

In other words, *Everything is God's will because God wills it to be so.*

There's even a simple explanation for those who are stumped by an intellectual impasse or two along this thought path.

God is beyond our understanding and does as He pleases whether we understand it or not.

No problem! That explains it so clearly.

That, of course, isn't an answer. This entire discussion implies many uncomfortable characterizations of God which are difficult to swallow but don't be too disturbed. According to Paul, we can be sure God will not deny Himself. He will not do things contrary to His character (2 Tim. 2:13).

Purpose, Counsel and Glory

It's true that purpose, counsel and glory are biblical concepts. All three are huddled together in two short verses (11-12) in the first chapter of Ephesians so there you have it. It must be true!

But before you start jumping up and down exuberantly, please note that first impressions and superficial considerations are not tools for interpreting any document, especially the Bible.

These are broad topics. Brief dogmatic definitions don't do

them justice and the nightmarish outcomes included in "whatsoever comes to pass" conflict so profoundly with the nature the Bible attributes to God, that it behooves us to think long and hard before supposing there is anything sensible about this definition of decree.

Calvinism

The heart of the issue, of course – what the catechism is really defining – is Calvinism. The Catechism doesn't mention Calvinism anywhere, beginning to end but there is a good reason it doesn't. The word is not found in the Bible.

The word is borrowed from the name of the individual who popularized the catechism's definition, John Calvin, but even though it's not in the Bible or the Catechism, it is widely used and encapsulates a teaching that puts a stranglehold on words that are found in the Bible such as *election* and *predestination*, and those two words are critical. How you interpret them will determine how you understand God's purpose, counsel and glory.

Those who wrote the catechism – Calvinists all – believe some very strange things. For them "the elect" refers only to those who get saved and they get saved only because God "elected" them for salvation. God does it all. The elect do nothing and only the elect go to heaven.

Of course, as you might have guessed, any person not included on the list is headed for hell without recourse. Begging, jumping up and down, carrying placards, shouting unfair and even believing changes nothing. Hell is your destiny.

Each person is either elected or not. God makes all the choices and there's nothing you can do to change them.

Not to worry, though. There are different and I would think better ways to understand these concepts, and that is the reason for this essay. If you're reading this thinking you are Christian because you are one of the elect, I'm afraid you might be disappointed. If you came here in fear thinking you're not one of the elect, you will find reasons for hope. Either way, may you find something to think about.

Let's start with Election.

Election Is For Service Not Salvation

I've already made plenty of arguments for this point but we need to consider election's meaning a bit further.   Just remember that every time I mention the word "election" I'm thinking service, not salvation.

"Election" Is A Human Word

The word "Elect" and all its derivatives are human words, coined by humans and used in human contexts. That's true of every word in the Bible and an important principle of interpretation is to observe the commonly understood meanings of words.

Don't get me wrong. I'm not questioning the inspiration of Scripture or suggesting the words aren't important. Every word is significant and powerful. God moved each author to write and then superintended what they wrote but none of the authors used a new or heavenly language. Every word in the Bible is, first of all, a human word.

If God used human language to convey His ideas, it doesn't make sense to change the commonly understood meanings of the language to figure out what He was trying to say.

Unconditional

But that is exactly what happens when you add the word

"Unconditional" to "Election."

"Unconditional Election" is incongruous. The two words cancel each other out. The word Unconditional is not in the Bible. It's an interpretive add-on that distorts the everyday use of the word election.

Interpreters employ the word to impose their understanding on the text.

From a human standpoint, "Election" in any language has never been unconditional.

Would any responsible person make choices arbitrarily? Do coaches select starting players without thought? Do employers hire people in the blind?

No!! A thousand times, no!!

We listen carefully, watch closely, read reports, assess and then make considered choices. And it doesn't stop there. Once choices are made, we continue to watch to make sure everything is as it should be.

That's the intelligent thing to do. Would it be wise to suggest God makes unconsidered, arbitrary choices about who to save? Can we extend the word "Election" to take on such implications?

Don't forget, though, that God's elective purposes focus on service, not salvation.

So it only makes sense to understand that elective purposes, which have nothing to do with salvation, are predicated on conditions. They always involve pre and post qualifications.

The Bible bears this out. Peter said:

Make your calling an election sure. (2 Peter 1:10).

Jesus said:

Many are called but few are chosen. (Matthew 22:14).

But that's not all.

Election Is Based On Foreknowledge

God knows everything instantly and at all times and his knowledge is the bases for the elections He makes. People are elected for service based on what God knows about them. He knows each person better than we could ever know them.

He knows us better than we know ourselves!

The detail of His knowledge is astonishing! Jesus said the very hairs of your head are numbered (Matthew 10:30). This is more than general knowledge. It's personal. Each person has on average 100,000 plus hairs. That's a lot of hair to keep track of and God has assigned a number to each hair on every person's head and knows how many will fall out before they fall out.

Not only does God know everything about each person, He commands that knowledge instantly and completely. He doesn't discover it or calculate it, He just knows. He doesn't have to think about it.

Self-Awareness

There is no comparison between God's capacity for knowing intricately and completely and the human capacity for self-awareness.

Self-awareness is a process. For some, it never clarifies, but God knows everything about every person, past, present and future, at all times.

And He loves us. God loves everyone equally so it would be impossible to say He chooses anyone indiscriminately. He makes fair and impartial judgments. His choices are based on all the information He has, which is everything, and includes bits we can't see or know: thoughts, feelings, inclinations, intentions and, equally important, future choices.

Everyone agrees foreknowledge is an attribute of God but when people try to explain how that works, the stories differ widely. There is a reason for that.

Why Explanations Vary

Although Election and Foreknowledge are both human words, each is understood differently.

"Election" is practical and material. Selections – another word for elections – between individuals are made daily. When we make the right selections, we are pleased and supportive. The choices who perform well are given raises and promotions to reward their good work and extend their influence. The ones that don't perform so well are vacated as soon as possible.

Elective processes are temporal, earthly, measurable and

manageable.

"Foreknowledge" is very different. It's philosophical. We're mystified by the future. It makes us uncertain and feeds our insecurities. We can't even be sure about the next five minutes, much less the next ten years, and we aren't happy with the uncertainty.

We carry insurance and create emergency funds to quiet our fears.

Or we resort to reading horoscopes, cards, palms or tea leaves or casting bones to gain an edge. It's nonsense, of course, but that's the mindset. People are desperate to explore the future.

Simply put, foreknowledge is out of our range. The only time we can visualize future events is when we try to force things to happen and even then there's no guarantee.

Coaches diligently prepare teams to outperform their opponents. It makes sense. Preparation is power so it's one way to influence, if not control, the circumstances but prepared or not the outcome is still a mystery till the match is over. There are too many intangibles. The difference between winning and losing can sometimes be nothing more than the bounce of the ball.

Omniscience Is Not Foreknowledge

Foreknowledge isn't a mystery for God, though. In fact, the word doesn't really apply to Him.

Remember, foreknowledge is a human word and applies to the human realm. God doesn't need words like foreknowledge because He sees everything at a glance. He's omniscient. It's a different word. The scope is far more reaching.

Events in the past don't fade out and events in the future don't appear distantly on the horizon. To use a bit of human terminology, God knows every detail in high definition at every moment. Every event for Him is both future and past.

Foreknowledge is a very human word. It's limiting. God employed the word probably because it was the best word to describe the divine capacity for knowing, which is far beyond our ability to comprehend.

Eternity

Navigating into the realm of things we humans can't possible understand is iffy at best but in spite of that we need to talk about eternity. Eternity is real but we don't live there. It's not in our realm so most of what we say about it is philosophical.

Eternity has no clock and doesn't pass like time. It just is. We coin phrases like *eternity past* when discussing eternal issues, which makes no sense at all. Eternity has no past. It also has no future.

Time, on the other hand, is finite. It has a definite beginning and a definite end. Time will eventually run out. Eternity has no beginning or end and will not run out.

Illustrating How Eternity Compares To Time

Think of eternity as the ocean and time as a submarine suspended in the ocean. We're in the submarine. We are surrounded by the hull of time and time is surrounded by the expanse of eternity.

We live in time, God inhabits eternity. We can't see eternity but God can see time from every perspective, beginning to end constantly.

The phrase eternity past is useful for us who live in time but only if we don't allow it to impose our limited time-based perspectives on God.

I agree that eternity is a difficult concept to relate to. We've never experienced it. Like the future, it's a mystery. But should we allow "mystery" to become a cloud cover for senseless ideas like God electing some to be saved and all others not?

Enter Jacob And Esau

You might be wondering why this is important. Well, it's important because the Bible states that God revealed His choice of Jacob over Esau before either had done anything good or evil (Romans 9:11). In fact, they hadn't even been born yet.

They were twin brothers but technically Esau was born before Jacob and was therefore the oldest. Humanly speaking, he would be considered first for the birth right.

God changed all that and not only selected Jacob for the

birthright over Esau but revealed His choice to their mother before they were born. That's very strange to us. The idea messes with the head. Time-based living gets in the way. We can't see what's ahead so we assume God based His decision on not-knowing too.

The answer to this apparent mystery is to see this from God's eternal, omniscient perspective rather than our time-limited view.

The reality is God revealed His choice in time but He didn't make it in time.

God doesn't make decisions before or after anything. Rebekkah, the mother of Jacob and Esau, was unaware of the evil or good the twins would do but God was neither unaware nor oblivious.

He knew that Jacob cared and would care. He also knew Esau didn't and wouldn't. And He acted accordingly.

David

I know you'll need evidence before accepting what I just said, not because what I said doesn't make sense, but because the opposite is so loudly echoed through Christian circles that it's now the imprint.

Not to worry, there is proof. David's example illustrates the point (1 Samuel 16).

David was elected to take Saul's place as king. Can I use the word "elected" here even though it wasn't used in the context of his anointing? Hopefully, you can see that the choice of David was an election.

Please note that David didn't get saved when he was anointed. He was elected, yes, but not for salvation. He was elected to be the next king.

David was the youngest of eight sons. He was handsome, brave and charming but he wasn't the strongest or tallest of his brothers. He didn't project the same physical presence. He was the least in stature and therefore less likely to be chosen by human onlookers.

This event highlights a human problem. We are limited by what we see and often make choices based on markers that are visible only to the naked eye. God, however, doesn't have the same limitation. He sees beyond appearances.

God's vision penetrates to the heart. He sees and knows

what humans cannot. Ulterior motives and personal agendas are not a mystery to Him.

And it just so happens that David's heart was the biggest factor in God selecting him to be king. Unfortunately, Samuel couldn't see his heart. From his vantage point, David's brothers were more impressive. When God rejected the first seven sons, Samuel was mystified and he prayerfully wondered about this. The Lord graciously provided an explanation.

The LORD does not look at the things people look at. People look at the outward appearance, but the LORD looks at the heart. I Samuel 16:7

What? God looks at the heart? Did He really say that?

Yes, that's exactly what He said and this incident is proof that God's elective choices are predicated on what He finds in a person's heart.

There are many Scriptures that mention this. David authored one of them.

O Lord, you have searched me and known me. (Psalm 139:1)

Through Jeremiah, the Lord made the point quite clearly.

I the Lord search the heart, I try the reins, even to give every man according to his ways, and according to the fruit of his doings. (Jeremiah 17:10)

In light of what actually happened and how the Bible explains it, one would be hard pressed to prove God made no consideration of Jacob's heart and future actions when He elected him over Esau.

I'll say more about Rebekkah just now, but Romans 9:11 was framed for the benefit of Rebekkah before the fact and our benefit afterward.

Foreknowledge Is Not Foreordination

Calvinists aren't convinced, however, and they have a deft work-around to obliterate the heart issues.

They suggest that God only knows what will happen in the future because He makes it happen.

In other words, God has foreordained or planned the actions of humans and guides them to execute the same. That idea is an insult to the attribute of omniscience but people don't often see this. It humanizes God and puts Him in a very bad light. It brings Him down to our level.

The only way humans can know what will happen in the future is if they manipulate circumstances to control outcomes. Manipulation often fails but that is how humans think.

But the above idea leads to the conclusion that:

God doesn't consider what people will do or how they will live when making His selections because He dictates their actions. They don't have a choice.

Again, the reasoning is very circular. Calvinists may not think this and I'm not trying to put words in their mouth, but they tend to use the terms foreordain and foreknowledge interchangeably. God foreknows what will happen because He foreordained everything.

Synonyms for the word *foreordained* are: made-it-happen, forced-it-to-happen, controlled-every-detail-to-make-sure-it-happened.

Arbitrary, Capricious or Worse

But, what if God didn't foreordain the things we do? What if He gave us a will and a set of natural and moral laws to work with and allowed us enough freedom to make certain choices?

What if we are only tainted by sinfulness and not completely incapable of moral judgments? What if ruination were the outcome of many bad choices and not the natural born state?

Calvinists can't think this way because if we can make choices and God knows what we will do and think, but doesn't take this information into consideration when making His elections, it would paint Him as arbitrary, capricious or worse.

He forces (ordains) one person to love God and allows everyone else to hate? If He can restore totally destroyed humans to an acceptable state but decides to restore only a few, there is nothing good to say about that.

Human Will And God's Intervention

The reality is humans make choices and those choices result in outcomes, a chain reaction, domino effect. Good choices result in good outcomes and unhappy choices produce unhappy outcomes.

What we learn from Bible history is that God's intervention is limited. He doesn't control the choices we make. He also doesn't prevent the outcomes. It's the law of sowing and reaping (Gal. 6:7).

The point is He wants us to make choices. It's His plan. It's His desire and it is the most important part of the learning process. We learn from the choices we make, even the bad ones. In fact, it's our bad choices and sinful inclinations that teach us about the need for salvation.

Admittedly, we may never understand events from God's perspective, but to believe God foreordained whatsoever comes to pass is the lazy way out. It's easy. No explanation or understanding needed. Just accept it and move on to the next question. But it's a difficult sell. People don't easily buy it.

Chapter 7

God's Elective Purposes Can't Be Manipulated

Calvinist have one thing right. When God makes an election, it is settled. You can't change it. You might interfere and make the situation worse, as in the case of Jacob and Esau, but God's choices can't be changed.

If election applied to salvation, the early American church fathers were correct. Don't bother asking for salvation. If you're elected, you're in no matter what. No invitation needed. No pray of contrition required.

But election has nothing to do with salvation and everything to do with service.

A few points from Rebekkah's experience can give us insight in the matter.

God does nothing in time.

Because God exists in eternity, He doesn't make decisions in time, on time or by time.

God's revelations are made known during the course of time and they occasionally foretell what's going to happen in the future but a good question to ask is why does He tell us what's going to happen if the outcomes are automatic. If He foreordained everything why tell us about it? In fact, if we aren't responsible, if we have no control over the outcome, why tell us anything at all, even the moral stuff.

God's interventions serve His purpose.

God does intervene in time but only occasionally and it's never about us personally. His purpose is always to promote His plan. He cares for each person individually and we are all recipients of His blessings but He doesn't pamper us.

God was testing Rebekkah.

One question no one asks is "Why did God say anything to Rebekkah at all?" How often do mother's receive direct revelations to prayers about their children? Do we expect this? Does God respond to mothers this way frequently?

I'm sure Rebekkah wasn't the first or last mother to ask curious questions about their unborn kids.

Keep in mind that this wasn't a mother's intuition. Mothers and fathers do intuit life trajectories for their children but this was different. This was God communicating directly with an inquisitive mother about the future of her unborn children.

Remember, too that this wasn't a conversation about heaven and hell. It was about families and nations, positions and influence, devotion and indifference.

So, what's the deal? Why did God reveal anything to Rebekkah?

Simply put, it was a test. The human response to unfavorable circumstances is manipulation and the situation in Rebekkah's family was a setup for conflict.

Rebekkah favored Jacob. They were close. Isaac favored Esau and since he was the elder, would have naturally chosen him to be head.

God, the third and most important party, chose Jacob. The election took place in eternity but was revealed to Rebekkah in time, before the boys were born. But again, why did God share Jacob's election with Rebekkah?

God was teaching us.

Maybe there is a universal reason God shared this story in the Bible. Maybe He wanted everyone to learn something about conflict and how to manage it when strong personalities hold opposing opinions about who should do what.

This wasn't the first or last time favoritism or sibling rivalry featured in relationships where God's will and purpose were involved. The first set of brothers, Cain and Abel, foreshadowed trouble. It wasn't unusual for heirs to murder one another to secure the throne.

Another good question to ask is, *What would have happened had Rebekkah quietly watched as the blessing ceremonies played out?*

Obviously, she didn't sit idly by. She got involved in a big way. She lied and cheated, and included Jacob in the deception in order to manipulate a preferred outcome.

But did she really need to do this?

Instead of securing the correct outcome, her interference made things worse.

Her actions made Esau's hatred murderous. It also fostered character flaws in Jacob that took years, and many bad experiences, to purge. Jacob's selection was secured for generations to come even if Isaac handed over everything to Esau.

Sadly, she caused a lot of trouble and all of it was unnecessary. Jacob's election was secure without it. She only made relationships worse. It isn't mentioned often but she paid a dear price for her manipulative ways. Once Jacob left Canaan, she never saw him again.

Power struggles were the problem.

This was a good old fashion power struggle and they happen all the time. Sometimes in families, sometimes at school and sometimes at work. Politicians are constantly fighting for position and sway.

Sometimes it happens over God's will.

Who is God's choice to do what? Who will be the pastor? Who will be the missionary? Who will serve in this area to that? These are important questions and God does have a say in these choices.

Sometimes we don't like His choice and do everything we can to avoid it. It's also true that we might manipulate the situation to make sure the right choice is made and justify any action necessary to see it done.

That's what Rebekkah did and it was the wrong approach. Maybe that is the lesson we're missing with all the prattling about election for salvation.

The outcome was ugly. The descendants of Jacob and Esau were in constant conflict until Esau was eventually wiped out. The struggle never ended until one was destroyed.

The blame for that outcome is usually placed on Esau but what part did Rebekkah play?

Before you engage this kind of fight, think about how your actions may affect future generation.

God is rational.

But getting back to the original question, *Does God take human actions into consideration, when He makes His choices?*

It's a fact. He knows that one person will believe and another will not. He knows that one person will serve and another will not. When trying to explain that, we must be careful. We're dealing with concepts that are outside human experience.

Calvinists suggest that God knows what will happen because God makes everything happen, but, again, isn't that how humans work? Don't we try to control events to achieve a certain outcome? Isn't that the mistake Rebekkah made? And when we attribute the same approach to God, aren't we humanizing God?

Election Is For Service, Not Salvation

Here again, we have two very different issues: service and salvation.

One relates to our eternal destiny, salvation. The other relates to here and now, service. Service includes our responses to God's leading. Service is what we do to further the cause of the Gospel after we are saved.

But we qualify for both. Salvation requires repentance and faith and is settled forever once we believe. Service requires appropriate acts of obedience consistently over time.

After many years of service, Paul stated before King Agrippa that he had obeyed God's call to preach the Gospel to the Gentiles (Acts 26:19). His comment came after many years of obedient service and would be followed by many more.

Service, the thing for which we are elected, requires long-term follow through.

I'm surprised I have to say this but there is no place in the Bible where anyone is "elected" for salvation and the proof can be found in one of the most favored passages on election, Romans 9-11.

The Book of Romans can easily be divided into six divisions:

One, Need for salvation – All are sinners (Romans 1-3)

Two, Bases of savlation – Faith (Romans 4)

Three, Effect of salvation – Peace with God (Romans 5)

Four, Conflict after salvation – Opposing natures (Romans 6-8)

Five, CHANNELS OF SALVATION – ISRAEL AND GENTILES (Romans 9-11)

Six, Implications of salvation – Relational conduct (Romans 12-16)

Note that election is only mentioned in the fifth division of the book.

Also note that Romans is the most comprehensive discussion of the Gospel. It covers everything logically and chronologically. Paul begins with the first principle – the need for salvation – and moves forward sequentially from there.

The first four divisions deal with personal, individual salvation or, in other words, the why, how and what of salvation.

The fifth division changes directions entirely. Here, Paul talks about service, specifically how did the Gospel develop and how will it be shared.

How shall they hear without a preacher and how shall they preach unless they be sent (10:14-15)? is the question at the heart of this passage.

This is methodology 101. The responsibility to share the Gospel is the point of this division and an important topic in the discussion is election.

The people mentioned in this division: Isaac, Jacob and Israel were elected to serve, not get saved, and Paul is encouraging us to ask the question "What part of this important task am I elected to do? Am I elected to preach, go, send or what?"

And more to the point.

Why would Paul leave "Election" for the fifth division of the book, the division which focuses on serving and getting the message out, if it really pertains to salvation?

The answer is simple. It doesn't, so he wouldn't.

One of the most clarifying passages in this division is found toward the end of chapter 11:

As concerning the Gospel, they (Israel – the nation) are enemies for your sakes, but as touching the election, they are loved for the fathers' sakes. (Romans 11:28)

The important observation to make here is that the Gospel and election are not one and the same. They are represented as different, almost opposing ideas. One is salvation, the Gospel. The other is service, election. They are not synonymous.

Election Is Broad

Everyone is elected. God leaves no one out.

Some elections seem quite glamorous: preaching the Gospel, going to the mission field, translating the Bible, but God's elective purposes don't always involve such high profile endeavors. Sometimes it's much simpler: teaching Sunday School, ushering, keeping books or even working reception in the church office. God has an elective hand in all these matters.

The point of I Corinthians 12 is that every Christian in each church has a different place and every place is significant. Everyone is elected.

Sadly, all the talk about being elected for salvation has emasculated the concept. If God elected individuals for salvation in eternity past and guarantees their salvation, whenever/however, no matter what, why worry? As Jonathan Edwards preached, *if you're meant to be saved, you'll be saved. If not, there is nothing you can do about it.*

Not only does this idea misdirect, but it also makes us lazy and completely obscures the idea of service. Don't worry. I know you can't earn salvation or even the right to serve but when God calls us to service, we can and should make a diligent effort to obey.

The truth is everyone is elected. We all have places to serve and each one is responsible to act accordingly.

Election Is Specific

Keeping in mind that election is for service, a good question to ask is what does God elect people to do specifically, and there are many possible answers to that question.

God might elect some to preach the Gospel. It's a strong possibility but a general calling alone isn't sufficient. It requires more detail. You must determine where He wants you to preach and so on. The possibilities are endless.

There are several important details to keep in mind:

No two people are elected to do the same thing.

Because elections are specific, they are also limiting. Two people can't fill the same position simultaneously. Isaac and Ishmael couldn't both be the head of the family. Only one was needed, hence an election was made.

And there was nothing unconditional about it. Isaac didn't earn the calling but he did qualify. He was the child of promise.

The selections don't stop there. Jacob was elected over Esau. Judah was elected over the other tribal heads. The elections in each case only involved one individual, but no election constituted the denial of all the others for service or salvation.

Because one person in each case was chosen to fill a certain position didn't mean all other potential candidates went to hell. How does any person reach such a warped conclusion? Forget logic. The idea is incoherent!

If the selection of Jacob meant Esau went to hell, we would have to conclude that the selection of Judah meant all the other tribal heads went to hell.

David was clearly elected to be King over Israel. Does that mean all his brothers – there were 7 – went to hell? David's brothers reacted hatefully when he exceeded them in battle. Can you imagine the reaction had his election meant he was being saved and they were not?

These elections were for service, not salvation, and

pertained to specific areas of responsibility. You can't fill one position with two people but there is a place for every person.

Jealousy can be a problem.

Jealousy was Esau's problem. He wanted Jacob's calling. He thought it was his, felt he deserved it and could never get over the belief that Jacob had stolen it.

He couldn't accept the fact that God made Jacob the family head. His anger festered into bitterness and the bitterness spread throughout his descendants. There was constant friction between the two families.

We aren't always happy or agree with God's choices and the temptation to meddle and fidget is strong, but the more time one spends regretting their calling, the more likely they are to neglect it.

Friction can be a problem.

Elections never conflict but people often do. It's inevitable.

No one serves in isolation so it isn't strange that elective positions will often rub shoulders. Billy Graham was a great evangelist but he couldn't succeed without the efforts of thousands of people working in close quarters. I'm sure there were frictious moments.

It's perfectly natural for friction to occur, inevitable in fact. Trying to avoid it is futile, but it is not okay to sow discord in back corners among associates to settle the disagreements.

We are each called to do different things and we will each answer for the thing we are called to do but we're also accountable for how we manage the differences.

Acceptance is the solution.

The biggest problem with election is not what or where but acceptance. Some people are elated when called to the mission field. Others respond despondently with fear and dread.

Esau was disappointed because he wanted to be the head of the family. What he wanted, he didn't get and he never accepted this. Does that mean he wasn't elected for anything?

I don't know what Esau was elected to do but, whatever it was, he never accepted it. Instead, he seethed in anger. He sought tearfully, but unsuccessfully, for a way to take the blessing from Jacob. He obviously missed his calling.

Esau isn't the only person to do this. Many have lamented the fact that they were called to preach or to missions or to some other field of service but failed to go. They still served and were grateful to do so but always with a sense of curiosity and loss wondering what might have been.

Elective Outcomes Are Neither Scripted Nor Guaranteed

David was elected to be King but that election didn't include polygamy, adultery and murder. Those things did happen but you can be sure God didn't ordain it.

The only people God elects are sinners. No other kinds are available and every servant, even the most obedient, leaves a trace or smear as evidence of that sinfulness along the way.

Sadly, all the talk about election for salvation has obscured discussions involving many important questions:

How can I serve? We're offered only a limited range of possibilities. Go to church, teach Sunday school, contribute to the offering, and live with all the rules. We need to think about this more deeply. Surely, there are many additional ways to serve. Not everyone is cut out for teaching five year olds.

What am I able to do? Knowing one's abilities is important to finding a reasonable area of service.

How can I prepare to serve better? Preparation for ministry is mostly focused on theological issues. What about accounting or gardening or using any of one's ability to just help out.

Theology is important but learning life skills is valuable too. It used to be that no one could attend seminary till they first obtained at least a Bachelor of Arts degree. That is no longer a requirement. Everyone is shuttled straight into Bible college and the ministry suffers for it.

We need to be rational. We need to get back to the basics. Election is for service not salvation and each person's service is limited or extended by how prepared they are to serve.

Notes

Chapter 8

Mercy Is Not A Synonym For Salvation

Mercy is a paradox.
It's never deserved
but it's never free!

God made a curious statement to Moses in the Old Testament (Exodus 33:19), and Paul repeats it in the New Testament not once, but twice. The first repeat is found in Romans 9:15.

I will have mercy on whom I will have mercy, and I will have compassion on whom I will have compassion.

Though the wording is slightly different, the second is in verse 18.

The topic is Mercy but this is not about salvation. The context is Service in both passages.

It's an interesting statement because it sounds restrictive, as if God is selectively rather than generously merciful. Makes it sound like some are in and some are out.

Interpretations vary but some take it to an extreme suggesting there is no rhyme or reason, no formula for who receives mercy and who doesn't. God shows mercy only to a select few and reveals no reason for the choices He makes.

When questioned, the answer is a bit smug: If you're lucky enough to receive mercy, be grateful. If not, sorry.

The Romans passage does mention two sets of brothers: Ishmael and Isaac, and Esau and Jacob. Even nations are named: Gentiles and Israel. And sure enough, in each pair, one is selected and the other is left out.

But what in the world does that mean. Mercy is a broad topic. It is expressed often and generously throughout the Bible.

The Old Testament taught that even animals are to receive mercy (Proverbs 12:10).

Jesus taught that God's provision of sunshine and rain unconditionally to all of humanity is an expression of His mercy (Matthew 5:43-45).

But Jesus also taught that mercy is conditional, that we must show it if we are to receive it (Matthew 5:7).

What Jesus didn't teach is that mercy is shown with partiality, that it is shown to some and withheld from others for no good reason at all.

We can't afford to generalize or speculate, but that is exactly what some tend to do.

Calvinism's Assumption

For example, the Roman's passage is often quoted to support the idea that God unconditionally elects certain people to be saved and abandons everyone else to damnation (Calvinism). In other words, He mercifully saves select individuals and withholds salvation mercy from everyone else for no other reason than His personal choice.

Forget rationale, the idea grates against decency.

I've made this point elsewhere but Romans 9 is all about

service. Personal salvation is not in view. But even if Romans 9 were focused on salvation the argument wouldn't hold up.

I agree, the wording is definitely restrictive. The context clearly indicates God is making choices between two options, choosing one and leaving the other. You can't deny this, but even the context limits how far you can extend the restriction. Choices had to be made in each case but the question we must ask is what were the choices about?

Many Kinds of Choices

Calvinists read Romans 9 and immediately think "Salvation" but that's not the only issue that involves choice. God made many choices just designing the world in which we live.

He chose to put trees in the forest, grass in the fields and animals of all kinds on land and in the sea. He chose nostrils for humans and trunks for elephants.

He chose diversity.

And then He chose to limit His choices by giving us the opportunity (not to mention the ability) to make choices of our own. He allowed Adam to choose names for all the animals and then accepted the names he chose.

God calls, and we choose to obey, or not. It's a choice.

Choice or Toggle

It is true that Isaac was chosen instead of Ishmael and Jacob was chosen instead of Esau, but it's worth noting that God didn't choose between Israel and the Gentiles. It was more like a toggle. He toggled from Israel to the Gentiles and will eventually toggle back, and the toggle was for service, not salvation.

God worked through Israel in the Old Testament and He works through the Gentiles in the New, but wherever the toggle lands, neither was condemned. Salvation is available to both Jewish and Gentile individuals at all times.

Metaphors

But even the other choices were different to what Calvinists say. God chose Isaac to be the head of a nation. It had nothing to do with personal salvation. Choosing Isaac was not the same as condemning Ishmael.

Can anyone definitely say Ishmael never believed?

We all agree that he was NOT the child of promise but does that mean he wouldn't, or worse, couldn't believe? How far can we take the allegory?

Is there anyone reading this article who wasn't a child of the flesh before they were born again?

The answer is obvious.

Ishmael was only metaphorically the Child of the flesh. He represented natural born humanity or, in other words, every person who wasn't Isaac.

Ishmael was no worse than we are and no less capable of believing.

Isaac, on the other hand, is the metaphor of transformed humanity, but the important point is their allegorical status was based on the circumstances of their birth and had no implications for their personal salvation.

Ishmael wasn't condemned by the circumstances of his birth any more than Isaac was saved by the circumstances of his.

But those very circumstances dictated the choice between the two. Could God have chosen Ishmael to be the head of the nation? Could Isaac be rejected? Was a choice really necessary or was Isaac the only qualified option?

Calvinists are correct in one point. Neither child earned the right to be chosen but the choice had nothing to do with salvation. Every Calvinist makes that assumption but there is no reason for it other than the need to justify the doctrine of unconditional election.

You could make similar arguments about Esau.

It's a stretch. One must be short sighted and obsessive to take the wording of Romans 9 and constrict it only to salvation and apply it only to the so called elect.

It all sounds rather ominous till you realize the passage is talking about service, not salvation and the two issues are very different.

Let's look a little closer at Mercy.

General Mercy

Saving souls is not the only way God expresses mercy. The

natural world is a daily reminder that He is both good and merciful: Good because He created it and merciful because He maintains it.

The Sun, the rain, air, gravity, the laws of agriculture and so on are all things we need desperately but none of us deserve. What we deserve is judgment but God has chosen to withhold that. We call that mercy.

Another word closely related to mercy is grace. That's the word we use when God gives us what we don't deserve like the sun, rain and laws of agriculture.

Mercy and grace work together. One can't exist without the other. Delaying judgment would have no benefit if we couldn't grow food to eat.

The Wages and Atonement for Sin

Historically, God provided more than creation.

The wages of sin is death, and everyone is a sinner. Sin deserves God's immediate judgment. Instead, God mercifully withholds judgment and provides not only what we physically need, but also the opportunity to believe every day.

And God even paid the cost for that.

John said Jesus was the atoning sacrifice for our sins (believers), and not for ours only but also for the sins of the whole world (unbelievers) 1 John 2:2.

By extension, that means that the people in the Romans 9 passage who Calvinists say were passed over, weren't. Each received mercy: Ishmael, Esau and Pharaoh. Each benefited from rain, sunshine, gravity and agriculture for as long as they lived. According to John, Jesus died for each one on the Cross.

Particular Mercy

However, it is also true that we are individuals and God relates to us personally. Some things, like rain, He provides for everyone, but other things He does for some and not others. The Exodus is a good example.

God mercifully delivered Israel from Egyptian bondage, and it was a great offense to Pharaoh and Egypt when He did. He couldn't bless one without hurting the other. Israel was lifted up, and Egypt's demise was inevitable.

Destroying Pharaoh and his army was an act of mercy. With

the slaves gone, Pharaoh's economy and leadership were over. How could he sustain the power of Egypt without an economy and how could he sustain a slave-based economy without slaves.

But the important question is could God be merciful to Israel without judging Pharaoh? Does anyone believe Pharaoh would have accepted a peaceful resolution?

If God blesses you in some way, your enemies will be disappointed. His blessing, though, isn't necessarily a zero sum effort. Blessing one person isn't the same as hating the other.

Mercy Is Not A Synonym For Salvation

Salvation always requires mercy but mercy doesn't always involve salvation?

God was merciful to Israel. He delivered them from slavery but this was not evangelism in the traditional sense. No doubt, some Israelites became believers during the Exodus, and some Egyptians too, but there is plenty to indicate that many didn't.

Collectively dancing naked before a golden calf is not what

you expect from new or long standing believers but that is exactly what some of the Israelites did shortly after leaving Egypt.

Opportunities Are Expressions of Mercy

The offer to serve requires just as much mercy as the offer of salvation. The great privilege of humanity is two-fold. One, we – as in all of us, no one left out – have the opportunity to get saved. What a blessing that is, and Jesus made this abundantly clear more than once.

Verily, verily I say unto you, he (as in any person, anywhere, at any time) *that hears my word and believes on Him that sent me has everlasting life and shall not come into condemnation but is passed from death unto life.* (John 5:24)

That's the first privilege. The second is we then have the opportunity to do something meaningful. Instead of being treated as damaged no-counts, we are privileged with options to serve.

God is merciful in that He doesn't hold grudges. He calls us to service, and the offer to serve requires just as much mercy as the offer of salvation.

We deserve neither salvation nor opportunities to serve but both choices are freely offered to everyone.

Paul's calling and ministry were opportunities motivated by God's mercy (2 Corinthians 4:1)

Like all opportunities, it requires a response (Romans 12:1). God shows us mercy and in response we present out bodies a living sacrifice.

Finding your place of service requires prayerful searching. It may take years to find it but the opportunity to serve is not only an undeserved privilege. It is also an expression of God's mercy.

Mercy Is Qualified For

Mercy is a paradox. It's never deserved, but it's never free.

Someone makes it possible for mercy to be shown in the first place. That's Jesus. His work on the Cross opened the door to heaven's mercy.

But human response is needed to ratify its effect. No one deserves mercy – if you deserved it, it's not mercy – but it always comes at a price. Jesus made it possible but there are conditions. For its effect to be enduring, something else is needed.

Paul was shown mercy in spite of his blasphemy because he acted in ignorance (1 Timothy 1:13). In other words, he had integrity. He did the wrong thing (persecuting Christians) but he did it thinking it was right to do.

God was mercifully patient with Paul, waiting for the right moment to confront the issue, but if Paul hadn't complied, the mercy would have ended.

Of course, we don't like to think that way. It's difficult for us to visualize a scenario in which Paul refuses God's call, but that is a possibility.

God's call is an expression of mercy. The very offer to serve is a merciful act on God's part but obedience is needed to extend mercy's effect. How one answers the call determines how and to what extent mercy continues.

Let's look at it from the perspective of someone who received and then lost mercy.

The unmerciful servant was shown mercy because he sincerely pled for it (Matthew 18:21-34). He later lost mercy and experienced full judgment because he refused mercy to others who needed it in the same way he did. And the point? Mercy is neither unconditional nor particular.

The question is not is God willing to show mercy to everyone, but is every person willing to access it?

Notes

Chapter 9

The Accidental Evangelist

It's Amazing How Many Elect Emerge When They Get a Graphic Glimpse of Hell?

I'm not sure what you would call it but the congregation's response to Jonathan Edward's famous sermon, Sinners in the Hands of an Angry God, was not a revival.

It was just one sermon and the response was highly emotional, to the point of being memorialized. No one then or now doubts the salvation of those who responded but a revival it was not.

Chapter 9

The situation was very unusual. Edwards wasn't speaking to heretics, hecklers or blasphemers. In fact, his hearers weren't even skeptical. They were regular congregants and they were anything but slack. They endured long, dry, complicated, and often irrelevant or condemning discussions on Bible topics every week.

Deadening, yes, but showing up every week was a sign of determined commitment. They weren't indifferent.

The services were probably lifeless – the effect had to be numbing – but we can't blame the attenders for that and there is no reason to accuse them of being spiritually casual.

Mr. Edwards was clearly a gifted man with a remarkable ability to articulate his thoughts. But in spite of these abilities those who heard him found his theology difficult to assimilate.

On the one hand he preached truths that were threatening. He did this often and no one articulated "damnation" more convincingly than Edwards.

When he described hell you felt the flames.

But on the other hand he preached a salvation that was

entirely inaccessible to man. He believed in, and again, articulated better than anyone the idea that salvation was entirely the work of God.

No human response – desiring nor believing nor trusting nor confessing nor committing nor choosing – could result in salvation. God makes all the decisions and does all the work of salvation and He only saves those He preselected in eternity past, at least according to Edwards and most of his contemporaries.

Now imagine for a moment what it must have been like to hear Edwards describe graphically the images of hell and damnation and to visualize yourself hanging over and eventually descending into such a pit while at the same time not knowing with certainty whether or not you happened to be one of the specially God-favored preselected ones and you were totally incapable of any response to secure salvation!

To call that emotionally turbulent would be an understatement. It had to be horrifying to listen to Edwards, a man with extraordinary ability to paint word pictures, describe condemnation while at the same time providing no means of escape.

Chapter 9

I don't even understand the point of creating such psychological trauma when the outcome is already decided? It's illogical. If people are condemned to hell without recourse why torment them before they go?

Many people did respond demonstrably to this particular messages: falling on the ground, jumping out of pews and crying out for help but who could resist. A sermon like that to the ears of desperate and sensitive seekers was like a needle puncturing an abscess.

And to further aggravate the situation Edwards' version of truth never allowed inviting anyone to get saved or encouraging them when they inquired. According to history he and others like him were asked repeatedly about salvation: "Can I be saved?" – "How can I be saved?" – "How can I be sure I am saved?" and so on. And being true to his theology the answer was always the same.

Go home and pray about it. If God is going to save you, He will save you and if not there is nothing you or I can do about it.

Because these questions were never resolved, desperation followed. In fact, the so called revivals of that time took what historians refer to as a dark turn. People became so convinced of their condemnation and were so uncertain of their salvation they became despondent and several committed suicide, Edwards' uncle, Joseph Hawley II, being one of them.

I can understand that response. Seeking salvation for an extended period without gaining assurance is enough to make anyone suicidal especially if the preacher is constantly droning on about the agonies of hell.

At best, Jonathan Edwards' approach was emotional battering or maybe we should call it bullying.

I'm in, don't know if you are, or ever will be, can't do anything about it either way and here is what you have to look forward to if you're not!

Not a very pleasant message but take heart, Jesus was much more positive and encouraging. He said:

Come unto me ALL of you that labor and are heavy laden and I WILL give you rest! (Matt. 11:28)

Jesus, unlike Jonathan Edwards who traumatized his hearers with visions of torture, pled for the downtrodden to come to Him and gave an unqualified promise of relief to all who do.

Chapter 9

Notes

Chapter 10

Choice, Yes Unrestricted Choice, No!

We have the power to make bad choices.
We don't have the power to make bad choices right.
We have the freedom to accept nonsense.
We don't have the power to make nonsense acceptable.

"Choice" has been relevant to every person in every era

and is part of everyone's daily life. You can't get out of bed in the morning without making choices.

Life's pathway is not pre-scripted. Moving from start to finish involves many electives and the ultimate outcome for each person is the sum of those choices.

Unfortunately, choice-making isn't fun and games. The difficulties associated with the exercise was illustrated best in Hamlet's "to be or not to be" speech and every major philosopher has added their two cents as well. Clever sayings abound.

Choices are the hinges of destiny.

Attributed to both Edwin Markham and Pythagoras

Hindsight is 20/20.

Author unknown.

And choices come in all shapes and sizes: easy, obvious, hard, intentional, blind, well thought out and so on.

You really can't escape it. You can ignore the issue but that requires a choice, a poor one. You can choose to rely on "chance" or live "under" the circumstances but that is like choosing not to choose. Another bad choice.

"Choice" is an essential part of human nature and history shows that it cannot be bound. Humans go places, do things, learn through experience, expand their understanding, overcome obstacles and become qualified, and all of this growth is fueled by choice. One way or another humans will exercise their abilities to choose.

Unquestioned Authority Opposed

"Choice" is the reason the Protestant Reformation came about. People refused to accept what they were told without explanation or obey inflexible bastions of authority unquestioningly. Trading our ability to reason for blind compliance is a choice human nature doesn't easily swallow.

During the reformation the idea that authority was right simply because it was dominant was rejected. Society came to realize that no one has the right to think, believe or understand for the rest of us and they chose to protest.

Tradition Rejected

The Modernist and Post Modern eras began in the mid 19th century and are characterized by the tendency to question traditional ideas in every form: religion, politics, art, and on every level. No ideas are considered sacred.

The individual became more significant and personal taste, feelings, perspectives or inclinations became prominent factors in the choices we make. The democratic approach in the extreme.

"Individualism," the ultra antithesis of tradition, does more than just question tradition. It endorses and encourages unbounded free thinking. This approach attempts to move the boundaries to accommodate whatever choices a person happens to make.

The fixed values of tradition are no longer accepted only because "it has always been done that way." Everything is subject to individual inspection.

The Question

But the question is: just because authority and tradition are no longer seen as guiding lights must all the choices they recommend also be recategorized?

Because authority figures couldn't give reasonable explanations or didn't allow for individual tastes does that mean the choices they recommended were wrong?

Should we throw out recommended choices or would it be better to vigorously investigate the reasons behind these choices?

Take, for example, the issue of sex. It used to be that just the discussion about sex, other than for medical purposes, was shameful and the inferred understanding was the act itself was questionable.

Even when general discussions became more acceptable, casual sex was still condemned as wrong. Then it reached the stage where casual encounters became accepted. Now, however, it is expected, which means, of course, that it is no longer a choice.

We went from having no choices about sex, for no explainable reason at all, to having different but still fixed choices about sex because public opinion said it was expected. Tradition and authority were traded for public opinion but nothing really changed where choice was concerned.

In the one situation we couldn't have sex. In the other we couldn't avoid it. Who's right? Fortunately, because humans can learn from experience, reason is prevailing.

Practical considerations such as unwanted emotional connections, unexpected children, unprepared for children, the lack of personal fulfillment and even disease put a break on the anytime-anywhere-anyone-on-demand approach to sex.

The bottom line is, even if you don't respect authority figures and the answers they give or you're sick of tradition and you believe individual choice is important, you shouldn't accept or reject any choice before you've seriously thought through the issues.

There is no such thing as unrestricted choice. *Consequence* and *choice* are siamese twins and the free and thoughtless exercise of your liberty does nothing to separate them.

Thinking carefully before you decide is a choice. One that is generally respected by all.

Individualism's Weakness

But individualism, though it has its good points, has its weaknesses also. It is a philosophy that teaches us to "take care of number one first." Obviously, number one for me is "me" and number one for you is "you."

There are places and times when that approach is smart. Airlines tell people all the time that should conditions require the use of oxygen masks, each person should put their own mask on first before attempting to help anyone else.

Individualism, however, went beyond a healthy approach to meeting one's personal needs. It began encouraging us to add new and diverse options to the list, deciding whether something is right or wrong for ourselves irrespective of anyone else.

That is how the thinking goes but that is not an accurate representation of the facts.

I would suggest that the idea of "unrestricted choice" is far less adventurous than we are led to believe. It is more a romantic day dream, the realities of which aren't easy to stomach.

Examples Proving Choice Comes With Restrictions

Many of our selections should be determined more by personal needs and the way we were designed than by experimenting with choice.

You might choose the particular foods you eat but no one, for example, chooses to need food.

You might choose to refuse food but you cannot choose not to need it. If you don't eat you will die very soon and get very sick before you do. You can refuse to eat but you can't choose to live without doing so.

And if you are an "eater" (every living organism qualifies as one) you have not always, in the genuine sense of the word, chosen the food you ate. You, like me and most others, probably ate what was available or affordable and that might not always represent your first choice.

You might have chosen the clothes you wear but you didn't choose "clothes wearing" as culturally acceptable. In most cases it is illegal to parade around without clothes and we can be grateful it is. Some of us are visually offensive fully dressed and even more unsightly when not.

You might have chosen the particular brand of car you drive but you didn't personally choose automobiles as your primary means of transport. Other people created the scenarios in which auto-transport was the best choice and they weren't interested to know how you felt about it.

You might have chosen the particular house in which you live but you didn't choose house dwelling as your primary means of habitation.

You might choose to love your birth country but you didn't choose it as your place of birth. And if it isn't the place you wish to live you might not have a choice to go elsewhere. Your options are not always open.

You might choose to be the best of what you can be but you cannot choose to be what you are not.

All the choices we make are not completely without limits. We wear the clothes we can afford. We drive the cars we are able to pay for and we buy the houses our budgets will allow. Unrestricted choice is really just a pipe dream.

If you chose to buy a house above your means, the bank would choose not to give you a loan, which means the choices one person can make is often determined by others.

I haven't noticed many Mazerottis, Lambourginis, Ferraris or Porches in most public parking areas. If everyone chose only what they wanted wouldn't those cars and others like them be well represented?

People don't choose the person they marry. You may have chosen to marry the person to whom you are married but that is different to deliberately choosing that particular person instead of all others.

No one makes an absolute choice unless they have carefully eliminated all other possible choices before making a final decision. People marry whoever happens to be in the way and sometimes become disenchanted later.

I am not suggesting we shouldn't be selective but even on our best days the selection process can never be entirely thorough.

If we were really free to make our own choices, I am sure large numbers of individuals would be living in a palace surrounded by servants. And in a perfect world where absolute choice reigns would servants choose to serve?

Yea, right!

The truth is, we are not free to make unrestricted choices and the choices we are free to make we don't always appreciate.

We can choose to be thankful for the food we have even when it isn't what we want.

We can choose to be grateful for the transportation we have even when it is rusty and has lost its luster. We could also choose to take better care.

We can choose to be in control of our finances even when our finances don't allow us all the luxuries we might wish.

We can choose to love the person we married after we discover the blemishes that weren't apparent on the day we married – within reason, of course.

We can choose to make the most of the job we have until we can qualify for the job we prefer.

All of these are legitimate, character building, life changing choices. These are the real choices we make. These represent responsible, moral, realistic and disciplined choices and we should be grateful that God has given us the liberty to make them.

Unrestricted choice is not an option. Do not confuse the choices we make with the choices we wish we could make. Do not be distracted by options which are not true choices.

You can operate outside proper "choice" boundaries but that is not the same as moving the boundary or changing the consequences for transgressing. We have the freedom to make bad choices, we don't have the power to make bad choices legitimate.

There is another choice which I haven't mentioned. One that every person will make and that is, we can choose to believe in God and love Him or disbelieve in God and disregard Him but that won't make Him disappear or go away.

Anyone, anywhere, at any time, under any circumstance can choose to believe in Christ for salvation and many have. Some haven't but the offer stands.

But, not to worry. Whatever your choice, God will not react negatively.

In fact, the biggest differences between God and every other philosopher are:

One, God doesn't take it personal when you don't at first

see His point. He knows that we don't easily get it and understands our tendency to experiment with the data.

In some ways He even encourages this tendency. How can we learn fully if we don't try and fail. God does not want us to be spectators or robots and He patiently awaits our wakening to the truth.

Another way in which God differs from all others is the fact that He will be there when things fall apart. He expects a few bruises along the way and allows for, even plans for, recovery. The only failure God doesn't have an answer for is refusing to admit failure.

It's like being alcoholic. You can't address the problem if you don't first admit it.

Being all-knowing, God always has the right answer but He doesn't pronounce judgment on our failure. He sees it as an opportunity for learning and growth and encourages it.

So, if you've made bad choices, join the crowd. We've all done it.

If you are still wishing for choices you can't possibly live up to, get real. If you aren't sure what that looks like, watch the singing trials on The X-Factor or Idols.

Chapter 10

Once you've tried and failed enough, choose God. He's always there and He's always waiting. And remember, worship isn't a choice. Who or what you worship is.

Notes

Chapter 11

Differences Between Calvinism And Arminianism

Today's Calvinists Are Different To Yesterday's

Either/Or
Neither/Nor
What Are You
Going To Be

I consider myself neither Calvinist nor Arminian and some would think I'm a mix of the two.

I don't mean to sound uncommitted or indecisive. It's just difficult for me to think any person could really side completely with either, especially since both are in a constant state of change.

Not only do the two ideas differ one from the other but the vagaries and varieties within each are also extensive. Once you think you've got a handle on one, a new version pops up.

I doubt any person in either camp today is exactly what the forebears of either belief were in the past. Which, of course, means that if you say you are a Calvinist now, you will be differing with Calvinists of yesteryear.

As things move forward, and we think more deeply about our beliefs, perspective changes. That's natural and to be expected.

But don't overreact to that idea. I didn't say belief changes. I said perspective changes. If it doesn't, you're standing still.

It's a fact. Today's Calvinists are different.

The same could be said of Arminians but does anyone ever talk about Arminianism other than Calvinists.

Chapter 11

Of the two ideas, the one most talked about, studied, explained and argued over is Calvinism. Everyone tunes into that conversation. Arminianism, however, gets most of its attention from Calvinists.

Whenever a person argues against Calvinism, they're immediately accused of being Arminian as if that's the only other option and it somehow proves Calvinism. It's not an argument. Ideas about how God works with humanity can't be dichotomized. One wrong idea is not proof that another wrong idea is correct.

If you say you're a Calvinist, what kind are you? Which part of TULIP do you accept? Which part do you reject? Of those you accept, how does your understanding differ from other Calvinists on those particular points?

That's true of Arminianism too.

The point is there is no mainstream either way. Saying you agree or disagree with Calvinism doesn't answer the question.

So, I decided to put together a comparison of the two. Actually more a caricature of the two for humorous effect. Don't get upset. No insult is intended. The following list of comparisons is not exhaustive and is written in the spirit of fun and humor. So, how do the two compare.

Calvinists are pleased to be called Calvinists. Arminians aren't really Arminians.

Calvinists who preach Calvinism bear little fruit. Arminians who preach Arminianism bear even less.

Calvinists are clever. Arminians don't have to be.

Children of Calvinists are always elected and usually very cardboard-cutout-ish. Children of Arminians are like a box of chocolates.

Calvinists love the people who love their ideas. Arminians love everyone generally and no one in particular.

Calvinists must explain why they are Calvinists. Arminians don't really understand the question.

Calvinists don't know how they got saved. Arminians aren't sure they are.

Calvinists fellowship with other Calvinists, mostly. Arminians will talk to anyone at the pub.

Calvinists are elitists. Arminians are universalists.

Calvinists believe God controls everything. Arminians believe God controls everything but them.

Calvinists are given genuine faith. Arminians are easy.

Calvinists are completely saved but never perfect. Arminians are never saved until they are perfect.

Calvinists love Jesus the Judge. Arminians love Jesus the Savior.

Calvinists have the truth. Arminians are still looking.

Calvinists try to make the world like them. Arminians try to make the world more attractive.

Calvinism refutes Arminianism. Arminians aren't listening.

Calvinists feed off Arminian pushback. Arminians aren't pushing.

Calvinists don't worry about the lost. Arminians are maniacal.

Calvinists think anyone not a Calvinist is Arminian.

Arminians don't call people names.

It's hyperbole. Don't take this seriously. If you're of a Calvinist mindset, smile. If you're Arminian, enjoy the pictures.

Chapter 11

Notes

ABOUT THE AUTHOR

Ennis B. Pepper Jr. holds a Graduate of Theology degree from Baptist Bible College - Springfield, MO and a Bachelor of Biblical Studies from Bethany Bible College - Dothan, AL. He wrote weekly sermons during thirty plus years of full-time ministry, contributed articles for community publication, wrote several booklets on religious topics and published two previous books, one on Divorce and one on Tithing. Though retired, he's still writing and this book is his third published work.

Ennis was born and raised in Jacksonville, FL His wife of 50 years hails from Knoxville, TN and they served as missionaries to South Africa for 35 years, 33 of which were in country. They have two sons and four grandchildren and now reside in Charlotte, NC.

During their years of ministry, they traveled to many beautiful places and had many memorable experiences. Consequently, instead of doing more of the same, they decided to do something crazy in their retirement and started a business, Bargain Momma LLC. They aren't independently wealthy yet, but are still having fun and wouldn't change a thing.

Along with speaking/teaching in church when the occasion arises, Ennis still maintains his blog, nowthinkaboutit.com on which he shares his perspective on whatever topic strikes his fancy. His ideas are neither traditional nor mainstream but are deeply considered and clearly expressed (he hopes).

Other Books By The Author

In Defense of Divorce: Why A Marriage Should Never Be Saved At The Expense Of A Life.

Tithing For Today: Why Tithing Is Good For Everyone In Every Era.

Made in the USA
Monee, IL
04 January 2024

50992720R00146